To Marian
Best wishes
from
Oliver Leech

CONSCIOUSNESS MATTERS

AN ENQUIRY INTO THE ORIGIN OF CONSCIOUSNESS

OLIVER LEECH

YOUCAXTON PUBLICATIONS
OXFORD & SHREWSBURY

ISBN 978-1-911175-82-7
Printed and bound in Great Britain.
Published by YouCaxton Publications 2017

YouCaxton Publications
enquiries@youcaxton.co.uk

consciousnessmatters@gmail.com

ACKNOWLEDGEMENTS

I am very grateful to my parents for encouraging me from an early age to question and to think, and to all those with whom I have shared a philosophical quest over many years.

I owe a great deal to Professor David Cockburn of Lampeter University whose wide-ranging subject knowledge and concern for philosophical standards led me in new directions and helped me overcome many an obstacle in the preparation of the MPhil thesis on which this book is based.

Most of all I am indebted to my wife, Lyn, whose support in so many ways was and is invaluable.

PREFACE

In what spirit is a book written? In the case of philosophy books there is a range of answers to this question. At one extreme is an expectation that the book is the definitive discussion of the topic and as such the final word. No more needs to be said. Tick the problem off the list and move on to another. At the other extreme a book is tentatively launched as a set of suggestions and possibilities with an acknowledgement that this is the best that can be achieved given the limitations of the author. *Consciousness Matters* is very much at the latter end of this spectrum.

Consciousness Matters presents a view of the relationship between consciousness and matter that invites discussion and debate. The author recognises that it is groundwork, no more than a partial and flawed contribution to an understanding of some of the vexed questions that arise in the philosophy of mind. It is very much an opening gambit.

It is difficult to think of a more pressing question than the enquiry into who or what we are: material objects, non-physical entities, a combination of the two, something else entirely? My own enquiries began with what seems now to be a very naïve belief that the problem might be resolved by study of the relevant philosophical texts and research. But, as anyone with experience of the academic world of philosophy of mind will confirm, the deeper one delves into such problems the more one is overwhelmed by an array of rival theories and explanations. How do you pick your way through materialism, functionalism, behaviourism, dualism, epiphenomenalism, idealism, to mention just a few of the '-isms' on offer (and not to mention all their off-shoots and subdivisions)?

The only answer that has made sense to me is first to try to get to grips with a plausible description of reality and then to proceed from there in a careful, step-by-step manner. *Consciousness Matters* is the outcome of this steady, plodding and low-key approach. It is for readers to decide whether it makes sense to them.

INTRODUCTION

Just stop and pay attention to the present moment.

What can you hear? The hum of traffic, birdsong, children playing next door? Are you hot, cool, comfortable? Do you feel the contact between your body and the chair? A little pressure here or pressure there, perhaps? Are there any aches and pains, a slight shoulder strain, a tension in the neck? Is there a smell of cooking, or polish? Now look at your surroundings: the wall or window opposite, the furniture and floor, their shape, their colour. Briefly put your attention on them. Attend to what emotional state you are in? Placid or agitated, pessimistic or are you pleasantly anticipating the next part of the day? Is there a conversation going on in your mind? Are you reflecting on something that happened yesterday, running through the tasks you need to complete today, commenting on your own or other people's behaviour?

We are conscious from the moment we wake in the morning until the moment we fall asleep at night (if not in sleep too, in our dreams). In fact, in a sense, being alive and awake is being conscious. I wonder how many conscious states we pass through in an ordinary day, all the changing scenes of shapes and colours we see, the rise and fall of each new sound, the variety of tastes in the food we eat, the many surfaces and textures we touch, the smell of toast, petrol, perfume and so on. And the little surges of excitement, the slumps into momentary grumpiness and the plateaux of general contentment or gnawing anxiety. And then there is the buzz of thoughts and internal chattering that never seems to stop. Even, perhaps, the occasionally thoughtful insight or deeper reflection from a more detached standpoint. Our lives are our changing states of consciousness. Over the centuries people have tried to capture the flux of consciousness in a range of metaphors: a stream of experiences passing before us; a theatre in which we are, perhaps, both audience and actors; a conveyor belt carrying a series of thoughts, feelings in front of us.

But only some of the time do we really focus on and attend to the consciousness of the moment. You are driving along an everyday route deeply immersed in thought when — perhaps a cyclist has swerved too near or a child has kicked a ball in the road in front of you — suddenly you are called to attention. And then you realise that for several minutes you have very competently stopped at traffic lights, negotiated merging lanes of traffic, carefully turned several times, all without being fully aware, attentively aware, of your surroundings and actions. Or in unfamiliar situations, at an interview, in a new location, at a social event with people you haven't met before, you stop short, for no apparent reason touched by a slightly disconcerting sense of 'I am here now. How odd, how very strange that this is so' and you hear your own voice as if it belonged to someone else and see your hands moving as if they were detached from your body. These are moments, I suggest, in which we are brought closer to our conscious states; more than just being conscious, we become aware then of consciousness itself.

And we can think about consciousness too and discover that, to say the least, there is something very strange about it. First of all, being conscious is a state we human beings and, we assume, animals can be in but probably not cars, mountains, trees and telegraph poles. What makes me alive and conscious when a mountain is not alive and conscious? How is it that, when I stand next to tree, I can know what it is like to feel a breeze but the tree does not? How come the world seems to be divided into things like me that have consciousness and things like trees which do not? Even cameras don't really see and sound recorders don't really hear in the sense of having experiences of seeing and hearing. What then is consciousness? Can we explain it or at least make some sense of it?

Not another book about the mind and consciousness, you may be thinking. I can understand the exasperation in that response. There is indeed an extensive literature about this topic which has become a mini publishing industry in its own right with links to several subjects from philosophy and psychology to neuroscience. I can find on a library shelf, *Mapping the Mind*, *Philosophy of Mind*, *The Conscious Mind*, *The Mechanical Mind*, *The Metaphysics of Mind*, the ambitiously titled *Consciousness Explained* and the more modest *Consciousness, An Introduction* and *Consciousness, A Very Short Introduction* and these are only a fraction of the texts I could access on the many internet resources for the subject. And there are also, these days, in addition to the vast literature, blogs, web sites and web courses on the mind and consciousness. There are probably evening classes too somewhere. Do we need any more views on these over-exposed topics?

The published writing on this subject seems to me to fall into two main types. The vast majority of books, like the few listed above, are serious academic works written by well-qualified experts. Whether the background is philosophical, psychological or scientific, they share a common viewpoint which might be summarised as follows. Reality is the physical universe containing galaxies, atoms and everything in between from planets to microbes, mountain ranges to human brains. The physical universe obeys natural laws (like the law of conservation of mass and energy) and is moved by natural forces (like gravity or the electromagnetic force). Furthermore, the physical universe is observable, quantifiable and open to scientific and logical enquiry. In short, according to this view everything that exists is physical or, at least, can be explained in physical terms.

Let me call this the Physical-First approach. From this viewpoint the mind and consciousness represent problems and are, therefore, the subject of an as yet unresolved enquiry. The aim of investigations is to identify the place of mind and consciousness within the physical universe which is taken to be a given and well understood area of knowledge. You will find here a wide range of responses: from advocates of a 100% materialism (some of whom even urge us to eliminate all talk of consciousness) to the so-called 'mysterians' who argue that, though there is nothing supernatural about consciousness, nothing that requires us to doubt the Physical-First assumptions, the problem of explaining the mind and consciousness in terms of the physical world is and will always remain beyond the powers of the human intellect. A much smaller number of books does not take for granted that the physical world is the fundamental ground of reality but regards consciousness itself as the point of departure for the enquiry, and not with a view to discovering its place in nature but as the focus of study for its own sake. Let me call this the Consciousness-First approach. It is more likely than the first approach to align itself with a traditions of thought in ancient philosophy and religious scriptures. While respecting science it does not see the scientific approach as the most significant or reliable path to truth. Needless to say the Physical-First writers, based in the world of universities, academic periodicals and conferences, tend to be dismissive of the Consciousness-First writers. In fact, that alternative position is rarely, if at all, mentioned in their discourse. They pride themselves on the logical rigour of their methods and are deeply suspicious of claims that cannot be verified according to agreed criteria. Anything that smacks of the woolly, the vague or the pretentious is out-of-bounds. The Consciousness-First writers probably regard the other group, however, as blinkered and excessively hidebound by a left-brain mindset that is unable to see the more holistic picture in which the physical is not the whole but a part of reality.

But before taking this rivalry further I need to do some defining of terms. What after all is consciousness and what is the mind?

Consciousness is a particularly difficult term to pin down. Some words just defy any attempt to define them. If I don't know the meaning of the word 'matryoshka', I look it up in the dictionary and read that it is 'a hollow doll containing a series of smaller dolls, fitting one within the other'. I can put together ideas I already understand like 'doll' and 'hollow' and easily learn the new word. Some words, however, present more of a problem. In the case of colour words, for example, like 'red' or 'green', the dictionary is unable to give such a breakdown into component parts and resorts to the use of examples: red is 'the colour of blood', green 'the colour of grass' and so on. There is something elemental about colour vocabulary that resists an easy dictionary definition.

Trying to define consciousness is even more difficult. If I were making an effort to understand colours I was unsure of, colours like mauve, magenta or tope, at least I would already have in my mind a clear concept of what is meant by a colour word. But with consciousness not even that can be taken for granted. Anyway, here is my best take on what the word consciousness means to me.

Consciousness is direct, immediate, private experience that occupies the present moment; it manifests in many forms. Consciousness is pain that might be throbbing or a sharp twinge or excruciating or dull; it is the experience of the senses, not just the famous five, seeing, hearing, smelling, tasting and touching, but also those mentioned less often like hunger, nausea, balance and dizziness; it is the experience of enjoying or enduring a memory; it is emotion directly felt like being angry or embarrassed or joyful or in a panic; and states of thinking like the moment when an idea clicks as we understand something for the first time or the experience of calculating a sum of figures when we hear the numbers one after another.

The mind (or the mental) I take to be a wider term that includes consciousness but contains more than consciousness. For example, the mind includes what we know and believe but are not immediately conscious of. There are very many objects of knowledge in this category. I know the names of my uncles and aunts and of the last five prime ministers but, most of the time, they are not occupying my consciousness; they are not in the present moment of my experience. I believe many things too, for example, that it will go darker tonight and that I have a heart and lungs but again these beliefs are hardly in the forefront of consciousness. I couldn't even begin to count how many items are in this category of what I know or believe. I think of them as a vast crowd of actors waiting behind a curtain for the moment when they may be called on stage and appear in the full spotlight of consciousness. Ask me who was the last prime minister but one or what is beating inside my chest and I get quick access to that knowledge and tell you right away. The comparison between consciousness and a theatre, by the way, goes back at least to the French philosopher, René Descartes (1596-1650), and is still being adapted to give an insight into consciousness in current studies.

When introduced to some of the problems of mind and consciousness, many people dismiss them as remote from their lives and as very difficult and abstruse academic topics to be left to experts to explore. These studies certainly are serious disciplines in university philosophy and psychology departments. But in my view the question of consciousness in particular is so direct, immediate and pressing that we cannot afford to delegate it to others. It strikes right at the heart of what it is to be alive — to feel, to think, to have experiences, to be conscious, is after all what every moment of our lives consists of. Furthermore, an enquiry into consciousness may have implications that overlap with other questions of serious concern to all of us. If I am interested in knowing what I am, a complicated lump of matter or something more, if I am interested to know whether the existence of me begins and ends with the existence of my body, then consciousness is my problem too.

Contents

CHAPTER ONE

PAIN AND VISION

THE PROBLEM OF PAIN

Bleary-eyed first thing in the morning George stubs his toe on the bathroom door. His face contorts, he winces, perhaps he utters an expletive, he rubs his toe. Nothing special here. An everyday event in many households around the world. Now analyse the event. Follow through the process from the cause, the contact between soft flesh and solid wood, to the behaviour in response: the wincing, saying ouch or rubbing the toe or whatever.

It is interesting to note how such an event would have been explained in the past and to compare that account with one that might be given today. There is a diagram in the writing of the seventeenth century philosopher, René Descartes which shows a boy reacting to burning his foot. Without the benefit of a modern understanding of how the body works Descartes saw the process in terms of wires or string-like connections. When the foot was in close contact with the fire, a message was delivered from the foot along the wire or string to reach the brain. This description may seem very unsophisticated but there is something very obviously sensible about it. If we assume that the brain is involved when the body is damaged, then some account must be given of how the foot communicates information that the skin has been damaged to the brain. We naturally expect that there must be a line of communication within the body.

Before considering a more up-to-date description, let us look at an illustration of the general process involved. Think of those stately homes of centuries ago. Imagine a house with twenty or so rooms where every room has a bell pull with which to call for assistance. Each bell pull is connected by a wire to the servants' quarters below stairs where the butler can see a row of bells arranged along the wall, each one labelled with the name of a room. When the bell pull is used in, say, Room 5, the wire connecting it to the butler's room tugs at and rings the bell labelled Room 5. The butler notes the information and despatches a servant to the appropriate room.

HOUSE PLAN

Room 1	Room 2	Room 3	Room 4	Room 5
Room 6	Room 7	Room 8	Room 9	Room 10
Room 11	Room 12	Room 13	Room 14	Room 15
Room 16	Room 17	Room 18	Room 19	Room 20

BELLS

1 2 3 4 5 6 7 8 9 10 11 12 13 14 15 16 17 18 19 20

It is admittedly a crudely over-simplified comparison but, for the moment, allow that when George stubs his toe, in some roughly analogous way his brain receives information, detects which part of the body is damaged and activates a range of those muscles in his body which cause it to bend down and his hand to rub the damaged toe. His brain is doing the job of the butler, accepting information, interpreting it and issuing instructions.

While acknowledging that what happens in the human body is much more complicated than bell pulling in a stately home, we recognise that some sort of transmission must take place from damaged tissue to the brain and from the brain to the muscles which control the behaviour. However sophisticated and complex it turns out to be, there is surely a chain of cause and effect between the stubbed toe and the hand rubbing. It is a task for biological science to explain how it operates.

Now, it is important to remember that any scientific explanation of what happens will include only the reactions of physical objects (for example, the cells in George's body) and of natural forces that come to bear on them. Science can only accept as evidence what is observable, directly or indirectly, and it operates on the understanding that activity in the physical world is 'causally closed'. What this idea of being causally closed actually means is worth dwelling on for a moment. It is the view that when any physical event takes place there is a physical cause for it. No matter what it is: the fall of a leaf, the explosion of a star, the growth of whiskers on a chin or a hand rubbing a toe, that event does not happen out of the blue or by magic but as the consequence of something that preceded it. And the causal closure idea means that the something will be a physical event.

If my car will not start one Monday morning, I check to see if it has any petrol in the tank, find out if the battery is flat or the starter motor is working. If it is none of these, what do I think? I cannot escape from the belief that there is a cause that explains why the car will not start and that this cause, though I cannot find it, is a physical one, something to do with the component parts of the car. I do not assume that a neighbour has issued a curse on my car, that Mondays are jinxed or that I am being punished for failing to make a sacrifice of offerings to the god Apollo. All such explanations would be non-physical ones. I cannot help being brought up in a world in which we take it for granted and very deeply believe that every physical event has a physical cause.

Now it is perfectly sensible to claim that science does not have all answers to all questions. Scientists themselves are perfectly ready to accept that any explanation can be corrected by the arrival of new evidence. But we do in fact adopt the position that, if an event happens in the world around us, there is a cause which is to be found also in the physical world around us. So when someone bends down to rub his toe, it makes sense to look for an explanation in the way the body works and the natural causes that control cells and nerves and whatever else the body is made of.

Back to George and a more detailed and technical description of the biology going on in his body. The important thing is to recognise the general point that there is a stage-by-stage series of physical events taking place here. When he stubbed his toe, the damage caused some of the cells of the toe tissue to break and release some of their material. Other cells responded by sending out histamine and indirectly affected what are called free nerve endings located between two parts of the skin, the outer epidermis and the deeper dermis, which act as detectors of injury to the body. Signals from the affected area passed along peripheral nerves to the spinal cord and along two pathways to a part of the brain called the somatosensory system where the information received was processed. Next, the motor cortex in the brain sent signals down motor fibres through other parts of the brain called the midbrain, pons and medulla. At the junction of the brain and spinal cord the nerve fibres carrying the information crossed over. (For the left side of George's body is controlled by the right motor cortex and vice versa.) From here the signals travel the length of the spinal cord to the muscle fibres which made his body bend, his hand reach out and stroke the damaged toe. A stage by stage series of events, every one a physical event, every one linked to and caused by the one that preceded it.

Now at last I come to the point. In all this system of action and reaction, of chains of cause and effect in all their biological detail from toe to hand, where in all this is the pain? I have not mentioned the pain until now. Of course, stubbing your toe is a painful experience; it really hurts. But in this physical explanation of the event so far there hasn't been any mention of the pain.

What is pain? Where is it? How did it come about? What does it do?

Pain is certainly real enough. What indeed could be more immediate, direct, certain and 'in your face' than pain? We can talk in terms of all the physical features, of nerve endings, of information passing along the spinal column; we can go into immense amounts of detail about the process without once coming across the pain itself. Pain does not seem to be included in the physiological explanation of the events; it seems to be outside the loop of these physical processes. Is the pain to be found in the toe, in the brain? Where is the pain?

Let's look at pain from a different angle now. Imagine that George visits his doctor about a pain in his knee. The doctor asks him the following questions:

'This pain or yours, now how wide is it?'

'How much does your pain weigh?'

'What shape is your pain?'

How would he respond? He wouldn't know how to begin to give a sensible answer. But then neither would anyone else. With a ruler or a tape measure we can tell you how wide a pencil is or a window. We know how to use scales to weigh things. But what would we use with a pain? It isn't the sort of thing you can lay down on a table and put a measuring device alongside. And how could anyone pick up a pain and put it on a set of scales?

The things we see around us have measurements and weight: the vase, the glass in the window, the mountain and the moon I glimpse through the window. But a pain? Its width, weight, shape?

'OK,' continues the doctor, 'we'll leave those questions until another time. Try to answer this instead. Tell me where precisely your pain is.'

'I told you. It is in my knee.'

A week or so before George had his knee x-rayed and examined under the best scanner modern technology can provide. He has received the results and now the doctor is looking at the x-ray photographs.

'I can see a slight swelling here'. He points. 'But I can't see any pain.'

The doctor is becoming more and more frustrated.

'The last patient I had in here was complaining of a nasty twinge in his great toe though he had no leg below the knee. How can you people expect doctors to help you to alleviate your pains when you can't even tell me where it is, what it looks like, how big it is?'

When we stub a toe, the experience of pain is intensely, undeniably real. But when we try to think about what the pain is, probably after the pain has passed and we can reflect on it, we find that it is a very odd phenomenon indeed. It doesn't seem to have any measurements; it doesn't seem possible to identify exactly where it is in the body.

What a strange thing pain is! Perhaps 'thing' is the wrong word. 'Thing' fits the vase, the glass, the mountain, moon and a million other objects that include the human body, the brain and all the bits and pieces of which the brain is made. They are rightly called 'things'. They have measurements, so many miles, millimetres across or deep or tall and so on. You can point to them and say, 'It's here,' or 'over there'. But a pain? Is that a thing?

There are other, what shall I call them, items that resist being classified in that lumpy group of 'things': shadows and rainbows, for example, holes and, perhaps, black holes. But they don't seem very much like pain either. The point about a pain, a headache or stomach ache pain or a pain brought on by a burn, a cut, a blow or childbirth is its blindingly obvious reality. When you have a pain, you most definitely know about it. You don't need to think, 'Do I have a pain or don't I?'; you don't dither and deliberate about it or ask anyone else's opinion about whether you have it or not. And yet you can't actually show it to anyone like your doctor, for instance.

Pain is first and foremost 'transparent'. If something is transparent, it simply means that it makes no sense at all to talk of a pain that is not felt, a pain that is not experienced. Again we see a striking contrast between pain, a type of conscious experience, and a physical object. I have seen many snowflakes and so have most people. But I can easily conceive of snowflakes falling on a remote Himalayan mountain or on an arctic ice floe that no one sees. There is no difficulty in making sense of this idea. Now we all experience many pains, twinges, aches in the course of life. Unlike snowflakes, however, in the case of pains, twinges and aches we cannot conceive of them existing without being experienced. The very idea of a pain on its own, a pain not being felt seems to be a contradiction; even to entertain the idea goes against the essential nature of what a pain actually is. There is a joke about the absurdity of such a concept in Charles Dickens' novel, *Hard Times*. The unwell Mrs Gradgrind was being visited by her daughter who asked, 'Are you in pain, dear mother?'

'I think there's a pain somewhere in the room,' said Mrs Gradgrind, 'but I couldn't positively say that I have got it.'

Pains are not the sort of thing that can float about a room in this detached sense.

What about reports from people who in serious accidents or in battle suffer terrible bodily injury and yet say that at the time of the injury they felt no pain. There is a view that pain is present but that it is not being experienced by them. Again, this claim seems to contradict the central notion of what a pain is. Perhaps, in such cases, all times of the most intense urgency, consciousness is preoccupied with the immediate pressures of the situation and pain does not manifest as it might if the same injury were suffered in a more tranquil setting. To me it makes better sense to say that in these circumstances there is no pain than to say that there is pain which is not being experienced. Each of us, or in these cases the accident victim or the soldier, is surely the only authority on the question of whether or not there is pain. There is no one else in a position of advantage who has the ability to override the direct acquaintance with the pain that the person actually experiencing it has.

However, pain does usually seem to be associated with damage to the body. But though we think of the two as very close, they are certainly not the same thing. There can be incurable and life threatening cancers that are painless and, as we have just seen, serious damage to the body unaccompanied by pain. And, on the other hand, there are people who complain about a pain which their doctors, after all they can do to investigate, cannot relate to any illness or damage to the body. Surely nobody thinks that all of them are just over imaginative hypochondriacs. So, though there is clearly a relationship between pain and body damage, it isn't a simple and clear-cut one.

In this discussion I am taking pain to be a striking example of a conscious state and of the problem that besets attempts to explain consciousness in any of its forms within a physicalist framework. But there is much more to consciousness than pain — the experiences of the senses, for instance. The conscious experience of seeing, of hearing or smelling or tasting will prove just as difficult to explain in terms of the physical goings-on in the body. But before looking in particular at the case of seeing I want to run through five reasons for believing that consciousness is such a problem. Some are explored in more detail than others. Think of them as starting points for discussion. Do they or don't they persuade you that pain and consciousness in general is:

a. different from matter or
b. (more of a challenge this one) cannot be explained in terms of matter?

REASON 1: PUBLIC/PRIVATE

Pains are private to the person who experiences them; no one else can have direct and immediate access to your pains or, for that matter, to your sense experiences, to your emotions, your desires, your thoughts, memories, imaginings, in short, to your consciousness. Physical things, however, are not private. They are open to public view to be observed directly, scrutinised, measured. The body and brain are physical objects too. If George's brain is being observed in a scanner, his doctors can see which part of the brain is active under different conditions. Brains are usually (and thankfully) hidden behind bony skulls but in principle they are part of the public world open to public view. The screen showing George's brain could be on a webcam watched by people all over the world. But in contrast with George's brain, George's conscious states cannot be observed by anyone apart from George himself. If he is tasting pineapple, adding up a sum or feeling grumpy, only George knows the special quality of that experience. This problem will be discussed in more detail in Chapter 2.

REASON 2: SPATIALITY

My pen occupies a space on my table; it is next to a piece of paper, behind a file and underneath the ceiling. And what is true of my pen in this respect is true of all physical objects from mountains to ants. They all have a location; they fill a place on the map of space. Indeed, it is difficult to think of a physical object without also thinking of it being somewhere in particular. The parts of the body involved in the process when George stubbed his toe and then rubbed it (the nerves in the toe, in the spinal column, the neurons that are activated in the brain) all have particular spatial locations; each is next to, above, behind etc. other physical things. It is possible to point to them and ascribe to them a position in relation to one another

But the question is this: can we talk of a conscious state like pain as having a particular location in the same sort of way? In the case of George stubbing his toe, it might seem tempting or even obvious to say that the pain is in his toe.

But when we look at the situation more carefully, we find that the experience of pain only takes place when the brain has been informed of the damage to the toe. A painkilling pill does not influence the toe or wherever else a pain seems to be. An anaesthetic impedes the signals from the body where the surgeon will make an incision. Cases of phantom limb pain, that is, of well attested reports from people who have had limbs amputated, of their experience of pain in the limb that is no longer there, make the notion of the spatial location of pain even more difficult to pin down.

Is the pain then located in the brain? It may well be correlated with particular brain activity that is spatially located; it may be that when there is a pain certain nerve fibres can be seen to be firing. But can we move from

a. when the pain is taking place, this part of the brain is active... to

b. the pain actually is in that part of the brain, spatially located there in the same way that a neuron in located next to, behind, above etc other neurons.

We can try out the notion of spatially located pain by a comparison. Suppose George has a hangover headache at the same time as he stubs his toe. Are the two near to each other or distant from each other? Can we use any terms of spatiality in connection with them? We could bring in other conscious states here. Could a pain be behind, in front of, underneath, above, inside, outside the taste of pineapple or the vivid sound of an oboe. We seem to have a problem with pain and with conscious states in general. They just don't seem to be located in a particular spot in space. It is a problem that goes back to Descartes but you will also find it explored in philosophers of mind today.

REASON 3: EXTENSION

Take next another feature of pain. As well as not occupying a particular place, it doesn't seem to have any measurements. Of course, we are here touching on a distinction famous at least since Descartes, between mind and body. Whereas physical objects are extended — indeed it is part of the definition of what we mean by a physical object that it is extended — states of mind are not. A nerve cell is such and such a distance across and deep and in length. Can we say that of the pain? How many metres, millimetres wide is a pain? How much does it weigh? How much water would it displace?

REASON 4: DIVISIBILITY

This distinction can also be traced back to Descartes. A physical object, whether it is a piece of wood or a nerve, can be cut in two: in short it is divisible. I can conceive of any piece of extended matter being split into smaller and smaller parts as far as the physicists say we can go, to sub-atomic particles like quarks or whatever. But a pain — can you have half a pain? Is there any way that a conscious experience, a pain, a taste of pineapple, the sound of an oboe, could be split into parts. It is difficult to think of conscious states in terms of their divisibility.

By contrast, however, you might say that a pain can increase or diminish in intensity; and think of the difference between a dull ache and a sharp twinge, between a soft and a loud sound. So variability is something else that is different between physical things and conscious states. Physical things are divisible; conscious states seem not to be; conscious states seem on the face of it to vary in intensity, a property we don't find in physical things.

REASON 5: ENERGY TRANSFER

When water flows from source to sea, when volcanoes erupt and goose pimples form on my arm, there has been an exchange of energy from one thing to another. Any event that happens in the physical world requires the expenditure of energy. Now in the series of events from the damage to George's toe to the reaction of rubbing the toe there are exchanges of energy: the movement of George's muscles when he rubs his toe takes up some energy. A fundamental principle of physics is that at the end of any process there is as much energy in the entire system as there was at the beginning. Energy is neither gained nor lost in total though it may change in form (e.g., from chemical to electrical or kinetic).

Pain is real; we surely have to concede that. But it seems to have arisen without the expenditure of any energy. Pain is a mystery in two senses here: the problem of where it comes from and the problem of what, if anything, it does. If we accept the law of the conservation of mass and energy, then there is as much energy in the system at Time $_1$, the damage to the toe as at Time $_2$, the rubbing of the foot. Nothing has been added and nothing has been gained. And yet in the meantime the pain has taken place. If any energy had been expended in the generation of pain, then there would be a loss of energy in the system, a contravention of the law. If the pain, had been the cause of the rubbing of the foot, then there would have been an addition of energy to the system, similarly a contravention of the law. Again it seems that the conscious experience of pain is outside the loop of physical explanations.

THE PROBLEM OF VISION

Pain is the most vivid and striking example of a conscious experience. But conscious experiences come in many other forms. If we look at the senses, we will find that the problems encountered trying to understand pain are just as evident here. Let me take, as the example of the senses, the experience of seeing.

What happens in George's body when he looks at a scene in the countryside, a bird flying above an apple tree in a field on the other side of a river? Well, the story we are told by science goes like this. Light reflected from objects in the scene meets the cornea which is at the front of George's eye and which bends the light to focus it. The light passes through the pupil which is a hole in the middle of the iris and adjustable in size. (When light is intense, it contracts; when it is dim, it enlarges, a reflex reaction protecting the eye from light that is too bright and providing more light when it is difficult to see.) Next the reflected light passes through the lens which 'fine-tunes' the focussing begun by the cornea. (The lens too changes shape, controlled by a muscle, becoming thinner for distant objects and fatter for nearer objects.) The light, now focussed, throws an image of the scene on to the retina, which is a one-inch diameter collection of light sensitive cells situated at the back of the eye. These cells are of two sorts, rods which respond to black and white, and cones which are associated with colour. The cones, of which there are five to seven million, are themselves of three types responsible, chiefly, for red, green or blue. It is at the retina stage in the process that light is turned into a different form of energy, chemical energy.

It is clear that, first, in all the stages up to this point all reactions are of physical objects, of material things with dimensions and occupying space, and all make sense in terms of a cause-and-effect process. Second, there is obviously no seeing taking place yet. There is nothing at this stage that could be called a conscious experience.

To understand the point that we are dealing here with bits and pieces of body furniture, with objects that are 100% physical without a smidgeon of the attributes of consciousness, consider what these rods are like and how they work. A rod cell is a minute but extremely complex piece of biological machinery. In length it is three five hundredths to one hundred and twenty fifth of an inch. At the end facing the front of the eye and so receiving the light, each rod cell contains 2000 discs lined up behind one another, holding within them 100 million molecules of a light-sensitive pigment called rhodopsin. In a thousandth of a second light transforms rhodopsin to metarhodopsin, the first in a series of chemical processes which culminate in the transmission by a synapse to dendrites, the branch-like connections of adjacent cells, and from there eventually to the brain. What an amazingly complex mechanism! It is worth repeating that at this stage the process has no quality that in the remotest sense could be called the conscious state of *seeing*. At the retina was an image of the object of vision. Now, however, that image has been translated into the completely non-pictorial form of information within cells. It is all chemistry so far.

In the next stage of the process the rods and cones convey their information to the optic nerve which enters the skull. At a junction in the brain, fibres from the left side of the right eye join fibres from the left side of the left eye. The same happens with the right side of the eyes. On each side of the brain information passes along an optic nerve to the primary visual cortex at the back of the brain; this is a section of the brain about half an inch thick and containing about half a billion neurons.

In this slow-motion analysis of a process so rapid that we are quite unaware that it is even taking place, we are still nowhere near the point at which George is seeing the country scene. There is a great deal of processing to be done first. One task of the cortex is to separate the different objects in the visual information, for example, highlighting the bird and the tree against the background of field and sky and putting the elements of the scene into some sort of perspective. Another biological process takes the information of the wavelengths emitted by bird, tree, river and sky, to form the basis of colour differences. Others deal with distance, with motion and stillness, distinguishing between the moving bird and river and the stationary tree and field or linking the information with memory traces in other parts of the brain. But even at this point in tracing out some of the processes involved I am using words drawn from an exclusively physical vocabulary; all the stages are chemical and electrical reactions of objects with mass, volume and dimensions. Any reference to a conscious experience of seeing would be unnecessary and indeed out of place in this strictly biological account.

Described above is a pared down version of an amazingly complicated set of processes. This operation, continuous all the time we are awake with our eyes open, is a natural phenomenon of staggering wonder. But where is the actual experience itself, of George *seeing* the scene, in the midst of all this biological activity and complexity?

What I mean by *seeing* is the felt phenomenon of seeing the tree, field, river and sky. How does it come about? How could it arise out of the maelstrom of brain busyness? The explanation pursued above tells me a great deal about the operation of brain mechanisms associated in some way with *seeing* but absolutely nothing about the experience of *seeing* itself, of what it is like to see. It is this, the elusive and intractable conscious experience, which the biological textbooks understandably overlook.

It is very tempting to imagine that at the end of the biological process there sits somewhere in the cortex an observer watching a screen on which is displayed an image of bird, tree, field and river, an inner person on a smaller scale, a homunculus, as it is sometimes called, a tiny person to whom the whole visual show of life is presented. Unfortunately, there is no evidence of any such internal observer. In brain terms there is no command centre, no audience observing the edited film. And even if there were such an entity, far from resolving the problem we would simply face it again. For, if a mini George were watching a mini screen, an account would need to be given of the physical processes by which reflected light from the screen impinged on the eye and triggered a series of responses in the mini brain with the result that an experience of seeing took place. Clearly, this is the same problem presented earlier but on a smaller scale. The unrewarding prospect of an infinite series looms at this point in the argument as within the brain of the homunculus lives a micro-homunculus and within the brain of that ... and so on. This is no answer to the problem of visual awareness.

How can it be that a continuous visual world evident in conscious experience arises out of the electrochemical circuitry of 'a slurry of tissue with the consistency of raw egg'[1]? It defies rational explanation and yet it happens.

---

1   *The Human Mind Explained* by Susan Greenfield

THE EYE AND THE CAMERA

A clearer sense of what is meant by the consciousness of seeing can perhaps be understood in the contrast between what happens when we see and what happens when a camera takes a picture.

Consider a camera and how it works. Of course, the eye is far more complex than the most advanced camera but in some respects it is similar to the eye: it responds to light; like the retina at the back of the eye, it receives an image of what is outside it.

But the eye is linked to the brain and the brain activates the body. Imagine then that the camera is attached to a robot. When my eye and the camera receive information that a flower is nearby, the robot and I both move towards it; when my eye and the camera receive information that a bear is nearby, we both move away. My brain processes information received from the eye and activates my body forward or backward; similarly the robot's 'brain' processes information from the camera and activates the robot to move forward or backward.

Is there any difference between the two apart from the hardware, the eye and flesh in my case, the metal and plastic for the robot, that is, the structure of the different physical materials involved? It looks as though in both cases we have a similar procedure: input of information, processing of information, directed action. Is there anything else taking place in either of the two cases?

In both cases what happens can be described in terms of quantities and amounts that can be measured: the light has a frequency, there is a transfer of energy from the light to the subsequent action that can be measured and so on. But the conscious experience of seeing seems not to be part of the list of quantities and energy that can be measured. There is a quality about it that does not fit into categories of quantity and energy. If we could put together a full list of everything in the event that can be counted and measured, there would be an omission. It is not a full audit of the event. It does not include consciousness.

We have looked in this chapter at two examples of conscious states, at pain and vision. In both cases we have found a set of reactions within the body that make good sense in terms of cause-and-effect processes of biological systems. In both cases, however, we have seen that outside the loop of these causal chains is the conscious experience, an event which is real, definite, undeniable, somehow both closely associated with what is going on inside the body and at the same time impossible to explain in terms of what is going on inside the body. Between the physical events and the conscious experience is what is called the 'explanatory gap', a chasm over which it seems difficult or, perhaps, impossible to build a bridge.

Some of the features of consciousness, in particular of pain and seeing, the subjects of this chapter, are presented in the tables overleaf:

HOW DOES CONSCIOUSNESS ARISE OUT OF PHYSICAL EVENTS?

	PHYSICAL EVENT	PHYSICAL EVENT	PHYSICAL EVENT	
E.G. A) PAIN	TISSUE DAMAGE →	PAIN RECEPTORS →	C-FIBRES →	
E.G. B) VISION	LIGHT ENERGY → CORNEA, PUPIL, LENS, RETINA	LIGHT ENERGY → CHEMICAL ENERGY AT RODS AND CONES	RODS AND CONES→ OPTIC NERVE	

PROPERTIES OF PHYSICAL EVENTS: PROPERTIES OF CONSCIOUS EVENTS

	PHYSICAL EVENT	PHYSICAL EVENT	PHYSICAL EVENT	
1	PUBLIC	PUBLIC	PUBLIC	
2	SPATIAL	SPATIAL	SPATIAL	
3	EXTENDED	EXTENDED	EXTENDED	
4	DIVISIBLE	DIVISIBLE	DIVISIBLE	
5	ENERGY TRANSFER	ENERGY TRANSFER	ENERGY TRANSFER	

PHYSICAL EVENT	EXPLANATORY GAP	CONSCIOUS EVENT
BRAIN ACTIVITY	???????????	PAIN
OPTIC NERVE → VISUAL CORTEX	???????????	SEEING A TREE

PHYSICAL EVENT	EXPLANATORY GAP	CONSCIOUS EVENT
PUBLIC	???????????	PRIVATE
SPATIAL	???????????	NON-SPATIAL
EXTENDED	???????????	NON-EXTENDED
DIVISIBLE	???????????	INDIVISIBLE
ENERGY TRANSFER	???????????	OUTSIDE ENERGY LOOP

CHAPTER 2

PUBLIC AND PRIVATE

FIRST-PERSON AND THIRD-PERSON VIEWPOINTS

When George searches through his memories, he cannot remember any time when he was not conscious. This seems obvious: all his memories are of occasions when he was awake and aware of what was happening around him. And yet George is convinced, like everyone else, that he spends time sleeping and so there must be hours every day when he is unconscious and clocks carry on ticking. So George, from his own direct experience, is aware of time passing but he also knows that time passes when he is not himself directly aware of anything at all happening.

George has another reflection on time; he has a distinct impression that time moves at different speeds, very quickly when he is watching his favourite sitcom or playing fiercely competitive tennis, very slowly when he is filing away documents or filling in his tax return. But he is also quite sure that clocks don't move at the pace he is experiencing but at a constant rate whatever activity he is engaged in. (George is not too familiar with Einstein's relativity theories but understands enough to realise that if he is not travelling at great speed it has little bearing on this particular issue.)

George is also colour blind: at Christmas he is unable to pick out the red berries against the green holly but, when he sees other people point to the berries and say what a bright red they are, he does not seriously doubt that there are colour differences that he cannot actually perceive.

Furthermore, George distinctly remembers his wife in their courting days saying that blue was her favourite colour despite her present denials and the evidence of an entry in her diary.

Does George have a problem? No more than anyone else who reflects on his experience. He is aware of two positions, two points of view, that are very different but not necessarily incompatible: one is of the way the world appears to him, how he personally, subjectively experiences it, sometimes called the first-person viewpoint; the other is a domain of facts and objectivity, independent of his subjective angle and sometimes called the third-person viewpoint. Here are a few more instances of the difference between the two viewpoints:

- George is in a crowded room; he alone feels hot, at least one other person feels cold and a thermometer in the room reads 65°F. Subjectively, then, from their first-person viewpoints, different people in the room have different experiences of how warm or cold the room is; however, it is a fact from the third-person perspective that there is a temperature of the room read from a thermometer and agreed by all.

- George is trying to learn a new dance that requires him to spin round many times, very quickly. He becomes dizzy; he perceives the room to be rotating. As soon as he thinks about it, however, George accepts that the room is stationary. Rooms only turn round in your personal, subjective viewpoint; in the real world, in relation to the people in them at least, they do not move.

- As he walks along the street, George sees the sizes of people and buildings vary in accordance with his distance from them, the nearer the larger, the further away the smaller; in his dining-room what he has always believed to be a circular table looks to him to be sometimes round and sometimes elliptical; George does not question the fact that the people, buildings and furniture are of constant size. When he attends to how the world actually appears to him with objects changing in size as he moves, he is seeing from the first-person viewpoint; when, however, he considers the actual world around him consisting of objects that on the whole stay the same, he is adopting the third-person stance.

All this may seem very obvious. Why draw attention, you might be asking, to such an unremarkable feature of human existence? I hope to show that there is something odd, at the very least, in all this, something that will make us think and look for an explanation.

Most of us accept the following story about our origins and our present place in nature: that the universe began several billion years ago; that there were stars and then planets one of which is the earth; that if we look in detail at any object on this planet, we will find that it is made up of molecules and atoms; that vegetation, animal and human bodies are part of the natural world and that they too are composed of molecules and atoms, material that can all be traced back to its origins in the stars.

Now granted the truth of this very simple but, I hope, roughly accurate description, a question immediately comes to mind: where do the viewpoints we have just been considering come from? Particularly the first-person viewpoint! It doesn't seem to make much sense to talk of the first-person viewpoint of a star, a planet, a mountain, ocean, river, or even of a tree. But humans, somehow, do have a first-person viewpoint. George, as we have seen, has a subjective take on the way the world appears to him. How can this be? George's body is made of the same elements and, at the microscopic level, of molecules and atoms that are the same as those found in inanimate objects in the natural world. In view of this why should George have a first-person viewpoint? Why should the world appear to him in a particular, subjective way?

And that is only the beginning of the difficult questions. Here are some more:

- First, what is the relationship between the first-person and the third-person viewpoints? Which one comes first and which one do we really know? Does one depend on the other?
- Second, how is it that George's first-person viewpoint seems private to him and completely inaccessible to everyone else? How is it that no one else can feel, see, perceive his experiences as he feels, sees and perceives them?

It is the second question I want to turn to next.

PUBLIC AND PRIVATE

We all know the difference between what is public and what is private. Think of public and private property, a public beach and a private beach, information that is in the public domain and information that is private and perhaps secret, or again the public life compared with the private life of a politician or celebrity. Public implies open to everyone, no restrictions, freedom of access; private implies boundaries keeping everyone else out except the one or the few with a special right of access.

On Thursday July 5th 2007 surgeons at Papworth Hospital in Cambridge, UK performed the first public, live, open-heart operation (*The Independent*, 6 July 07). The operation was transmitted via a video link to a theatre auditorium in London where it was watched by an audience of all ages. A very public event. This audience was able to observe the surgeon take the lifeless heart in his hands and make it beat once more with the aid of a fibrillator.

There is no reason why operations on other parts of the body should not also have a public audience. Operations on the brain, for example, which have a long history. In the 1950s Wilder Penfield, a neurosurgeon working in Montreal, Canada, was trying to help patients suffering from epilepsy. He hoped that by stimulating the brain with electrodes he could identify more clearly the exact location responsible for epileptic seizures. His patients were given local anaesthetics but remained conscious all the time he was operating. We will return to Penfield's experiments in a moment. In principle there is no reason why they could not have been filmed and watched by an audience, just like the one that watched the heart operation.

Nowadays, operations on the brain and facilities for scanning the brain are much more sophisticated. For PET (positron emission tomography) scanning a radioactive tracer inserted into the blood stream reveals the brain's hot spots, that is, the parts of the brain doing most work at any one time. In the 1980s f-MRI (functional magnetic resonance imaging) was developed and works faster than PET. Most recently MEG (magnetoencephalography) has been developed, an even more rapid recorder of brain activity, picking up even very weak magnetic fields. Again, as we saw with Penfield's operations, there is no reason in principle why what is revealed about the brain by these modern scanners should not be watched by a public audience. After all the brain, like the heart and every other part of the body, is an object in the public domain.

Go back to Penfield's experiments. What he discovered went far beyond his expectations. When parts of the temporal lobes (sections of the brain situated at the sides) were stimulated by the electrodes, his patients — remember that they were fully awake during the procedures — reported having conscious experiences. These might be hearing a tune or remembering seeing a garden through a window. And here is the important distinction to which I want to draw attention. The conscious experiences that his patients had were private to them. Neither Penfield nor anyone else could know directly what it was like to hear that tune or see that garden through the window. In contrast, they could very clearly observe the brain; the brain was out there open to public scrutiny. The private, the first-person viewpoint, was somehow cut off from public view.

The latest techniques of scanning the brain give a very precise indication of which parts of the brain are active when the patient is having conscious experiences. But what we have inferred from Penfield's case applies just as much to scanners. Analysing brain activity in however much detail and accuracy gives us no direct insight into the nature of the conscious experience itself. We cannot by virtue of seeing part of the brain light up with activity know what the experience feels like in the way that the patient knows, that is, knowing at first hand, without mediation. Only the person having that experience knows the experience in the full sense of being directly acquainted with it.

Whether we are referring to Penfield's work or to f-MRI scanners, we encounter the same problem. However, detailed the observation of the brain, we never cross the barrier that separates the public from the private. And I don't think it makes any difference how sophisticated scanning techniques become in the future. If we knew a billion more facts revealing the workings of the brain in the most detail conceivable, would we be any nearer to understanding the relationship of the brain to consciousness?

There seems to be something odd and mysterious about consciousness that makes it essentially private, as if ring-fenced within the individual's personal domain and inaccessible to anyone else. And that quality, being private to one person, being exclusive, is not a feature of the brain which is in principle as open to public gaze as the top of a mountain or the Eiffel Tower.

How do we begin to make sense of this startling difference? How can it be that organisms like humans and animals which have physical bodies available and open to public observation and so are just like every other large scale object in the universe, how can it be that they have in addition this inner awareness that is out of reach to all but one experiencer, the one receiver of private consciousness in the first-person viewpoint? As far as we can tell, stars, planets, oceans, hills, trees and flowers do not have this two-sidedness, this separate 'inside' view. There is not a first-person viewpoint for a rock; there is no subjective feel to being a river flowing down a valley. How then can it be that human bodies and some animal bodies, built out of the same basic ingredients formed out of the same stellar debris as the rocks and rivers, have acquired this quite amazing quality?

It is an understandable human tendency to feel more comfortable with facts and figures that are definite and impossible to argue about in preference to whatever seems vague, subjective and wishy washy. Objects and movements in the public domain very obligingly yield available facts of just this type and allow us to measure them in terms of, for example, their length, temperature, velocity, mass. Naturally, since we want to be accurate, fair and objective, we concentrate on those properties that are public and so checkable by others. We can see this tendency to consider things in terms of their public properties rather than in terms of the elusive conscious experience at work in the following example.

HOT CHILLIES AND EVEN HOTTER ONES

The Scoville Heat Unit is a measure of chillies: the higher the number of units the hotter the chilli. The unit is named after Wilbur Scoville who invented it in 1912. By this standard a habenero chilli is hotter than a scotch bonnet, a cayenne not as hot as a Thai chilli.

At first the measurement was based on the people reporting how hot the different chillies tasted to them; as a result of their responses the chillies would be ranked in order of hotness. But asking people how they subjectively rate a taste on a scale of, say, one to ten, may be acceptable in a rough and ready kind of way but it is not a very scientific method of measurement. Better to have an objective test with the evidence in public which can be recorded in documents in an official way and available to be verified by anyone who might doubt it.

That is one of the troubles with consciousness like the actual taste of the chillies when considered from the standpoint of science. You cannot put it into a test tube, beside a Geiger counter, on scales to be weighed, alongside a ruler; you cannot insert a thermometer into it. It just isn't a public object like a bag of mushrooms or a blood sample. You cannot actually measure the something-it-is-like quality of the taste of a chilli. So, since you need public measurements to meet the standards required for science, you have to measure something else.

What can be measured in the case of chillies, however, is the number of capsaicinoids present in them. Capsaicinoids are a class of compounds found in plants in the capsicum family which includes chillies. Using this method we can, apparently, quantify the hotness of chillies and get rid of the unreliability of subjective opinion. But when the caspsaicinoid measurement has been taken and logged, do we now really have a record of the taste, of how hot it actually is to the person consuming it? It may be the best method we have at our disposal and it may well be adequate as a way to put chillies in rank order but I don't think that what we find out provides the results that really count.

We can certainly find a correlation between the number of capsaicinoids present in the chilli and the verbal reports of those eating them. But what any amount of reporting will not reveal is whether two people who, say, agree that a habanero chilli registers at point 8 on a hotness scale of 1 to 10, are actually having the same taste experience.

Consider this possibility. It might be that when George eats a chilli, his experience has twice the intensity of the taste Jane has when she eats a similar chilli. (Unfortunately, another snag is that two people cannot eat exactly the same item. One chilli chopped in two might be the nearest we can get to this.) George and Jane both use the same graduated scale, each rates the habanero at the same point on the scale. But, if George were to experience the taste that Jane experiences, it might only be point 4 to him. Of course, he cannot do this precisely for the reason that we can only have our own experiences and not other people's. The only person in a position to make a judgement about the taste is the one having the experience and there is no way of checking that against any objective scale.

An old eastern tale tells of a man who lost his key at night. Although he had dropped it in his garden, his friends found him looking for it inside his house. When they put this absurdity to him, he replied that he was looking inside his house because there was more light there. There is certainly more light in public domain where we can measure objects according to many scales. We get plenty of facts as a consequence (like quantities of capsaicinoids). But there is a price to be paid for adopting this approach. We may find ourselves overwhelmed with facts, with lists and lists on page after page of measurements, none of which have any bearing on the subject matter we are really interested in, namely, consciousness itself. Consider how very few words there are to describe the different types of pain: aching, piercing, throbbing and perhaps a few more – the vocabulary is certainly very impoverished. By contrast, there are countless ways by which doctors can measure and quantify the physical conditions that accompany the pain. Public events are open to the procedures of counting, measuring and so on. Science studies them and comes up with impressive and practically useful theories. But we mustn't forget what is not public within us and what other people and even science cannot access.

BEHAVIOURISM

For many years this pressure to study the mind and consciousness in terms of objective, quantifiable data found expression in a movement called behaviourism. In Chapter 1 we looked at an example of pain. When George stubbed his toe, he reacted in several ways: he winced, he swore, he rubbed his toe with his hand. Those reactions, or behaviours as they came to be called, were publicly observable. They might even have been captured on film. Behaviourists took these forms of behaviour to be, not an expression of pain as we might be inclined to think, but as the pain itself. To them it was a mistake to think in terms of the pain **and** the behaviour. What people meant by 'the pain itself', if anything at all, was outside the reach of observation whereas the pain behaviour was clearly open to view. They wanted to concentrate on what could indeed be observed and they dismissed the idea of a private domain of consciousness beyond the behaviour as a belief in a 'ghost in the machine', a fictional entity in the mechanical brain.

You can easily appreciate the appeal of behaviourism in the case of emotions. There are, it seems, six basic types of emotion: anger, fear, disgust, surprise, joy and sorrow and in all societies these emotions are expressed in much the same way.

The universality of facial expressions gives us confidence in identifying the emotional state a person is in, particularly in these clear-cut cases. So if George is happy, we will notice his mouth widen into a grin; if he is disgusted, his nose will turn up. But we must remember that for the behaviourist that facial alteration is not how he expresses his inner emotions; for them the emotion is nothing other than the behaviour.

But there are some very obvious problems in behaviourism. Suppose George has been reading the writings of Marcus Aurelius (121-180 AD) who combined the office of Roman Emperor with the practices of a stoic philosopher. A stoic philosopher strove to accept whatever happened to him, success or catastrophe, with complete equanimity, not showing any emotional states. Inspired by Marcus Aurelius, George could try to conceal his feelings: if he won a major prize from the lottery or he suffered a personal tragedy, it would not be possible to detect from any change in his facial expression what he was experiencing. It seem clear to most people that there is an important distinction between the feeling and the expression of the feeling; we can conceal our feelings and indeed we can dissemble, presenting false smiles and weeping crocodile tears for our audience. There have been cases of people later convicted of murder who appeared before the press in what appeared to be a very distressed state of grief as they appealed for help in solving the very crime that they themselves had committed. What is on show in public does not necessarily represent what is being experienced privately. Behaviourism rejects the private; indeed it denies its existence in order to maintain a commitment to objective analysis of what is public and verifiable. The price of this approach is very heavy indeed;

it requires that we ignore those very experiences that are direct and immediately real to us.

THE INVERTED SPECTRUM

George and Jane have a day out together: they visit a garden, tour the countryside, have a meal in a restaurant and go to a concert.

'My favourite flower was the buddleia,' says George in the evening.

'And mine the orange blossom,' replies Jane. She goes on. 'Suppose that the fragrance you experienced when you sniffed the buddleia was the same smell I experienced when I sniffed the orange blossom.'

'You mean that when we were under the orange blossom we were not enjoying the same smell.'

'Exactly.'

'But we both called it the smell of the orange blossom?'

'Yes.'

'So you are suggesting that the smell you were enjoying was different from the smell I was enjoying even though we were standing by the same tree.'

'It is a possibility. How could we ever know?'

George gets interested. 'And when we parked at the viewing point this afternoon and looked out over fields and the sea, the colour you saw when you looked into the distance.'

'The colour we both called blue.'

'Might have been the colour I saw when I was looking at the foreground at the fields.'

'That we both would agree was green.'

'Because I cannot get into your mind and see what you see as you see it.'

'And vice versa.'

'Remember the meal and the chillies we agreed were really hot. We both gasped as if our mouths had been burned.'

'But it might have tasted to you like the taste I have when eating mustard or onion.'

'And the music we heard at the concert.'

'I know what you are going to say.'

'Maybe your hearing-a-clarinet-experience was the same as my hearing-an-oboe experience.'

'Maybe.'

The discussion went on late into the evening. One of the consequences of the fact that our conscious states are private to the person having them and inaccessible to everyone else is that, even though we share the same vocabulary, we can never know whether other people are having the same experiences that we are having. Maybe, they are the same; maybe they are a little different in some areas or very different in many areas. How could we ever find out the truth here?

By the way, you will have noticed that in the dialogue above of the five senses one was omitted. They had enjoyed a romantic day together; it was now getting late. No doubt opportunities arose for George and Jane to extend their reflections to the sense of touch.

ZOMBIES

In the middle of the night Jane suddenly wakes up and sits bolt upright. She has had a horrific dream about zombies. These were not the zombies made famous in films, the undead shuffling along menacingly with arms extended and expressionless faces. Jane's dream was peopled by philosophical zombies including a zombie George. Philosophical zombies have human bodies. They look just like us and behave just like us. They eat breakfast and go to work; they grumble about the traffic and the weather; they swear when they stub a toe and go 'Mmm' when they taste strawberries and 'Wow!' when they bite into habanera chillies. In fact they are physically and in behaviour indistinguishable from us. If you analysed their blood or urine samples, tested their reflexes or scanned their brains, you would not be able to detect the slightest difference between a zombie and a real human. Cell for cell, molecule for molecule, atom for atom, they are exactly like us.

But there is a crucial difference, nevertheless. A zombie George has no consciousness. He does not taste the breakfast or feel irritated by the queue and rain; he does not even feel pain when his soft toe collides with the solid door or any taste at all when the fruit is on his tongue.

What Jane has realised is a shock to her. Her dream has alerted her to another implication of the fact that we can never get access to perceptions from the first-person viewpoint of someone else. And this implication is more far-reaching than the possibility that we may have different experiences even though we call them by the same names. That was material for comedy: zombies are the stuff of nightmares.

The point is this. We have so far been assuming that the conscious states of others, because they are inaccessible to us, might be different from our own. But when we really go into the question we find that it raises an even more fundamental difficulty. A zombie is a concept we can consider purely as a theoretical possibility. We don't have to take it too seriously in day-to-day terms but we can regard it as part of a thought experiment, a way of testing ideas to see if they make sense.

One obvious implication is that we now have a difficulty in knowing the difference between a zombie and a non-zombie. But, putting that aside for a moment, consider the following. If the zombie without consciousness is exactly the same as the non-zombie with consciousness, exactly the same in all aspects of behaviour, in every physical detail down to the last atom and quark, then what is it that makes the non-zombie (you and me, presumably) different from the zombie in the sense that we are conscious and the zombie is not? How could the difference be explained in terms of the physical world of objects, natural forces and laws? For in these terms there is no distinction between the conscious and the non-conscious versions of George. How can it be that this physical body has conscious states when it would be not different in any way detectable by other people if it had no conscious states at all?

The philosopher Saul Kripke asked a question that is very pertinent here. Suppose God makes the physical universe in its entirety including human beings with their brains completely intact and working. Has God at this stage finished his work or does he have more to do? The question is this: when he makes humans with brains that receive input and emit output, does consciousness, pain and so on, come along with the territory, naturally, inevitably? Or is consciousness an add-on, an extra something that requires separate creation? How you answer this question is very revealing as regards your attitude to the relationship between the brain and consciousness. The point can be made clearer by introducing a contrast.

There is a particular fact that is true of triangles. The internal angles of a triangle add up to two right angles. This fact can be easily demonstrated with a little geometry and cannot seriously be disputed. You cannot have a triangle that is an exception to this rule. You cannot think of one, imagine one, conceive of one. There could not be a place on any planet in the universe either now or in the depths of the past or as far into the future as you like where there could be a different sort of triangle. Having internal angles that add up to two right angles is a necessary truth about triangles.

But what about zombies? Can there be organisms exactly like human ones in a complete sense (atom for atom copies) which do not have consciousness? Although I could not conceive of a triangle without its internal angles equalling two right angles, I can quite easily conceive of a being as just described, of a zombie. It does not seem to me to be necessary that a human body with all its parts working and with a full set of a hundred billion neurons in operation in its brain **must** have consciousness. After all, I do not have any difficulty understanding that liver cells and lung cells are not accompanied by conscious states. Why then should it be a problem to conceive of brain cells, even allowing for the fact that they are a different type of cell, as not being accompanied by consciousness? Neuroscientists cannot point to a particular type of neuron or a particular collection of neurons which have a special function of giving rise to consciousness and the activity of those neurons makes perfectly good sense anyway in terms of the unconscious communication system of the brain. So there seems no good reason to claim that consciousness does in fact come along with the territory of brains, that it is a necessary property of brains in the way that triangles have necessary properties. Quite the reverse in fact. There is not the slightest reason why a complex of cells should have any connection whatsoever with conscious experiences.

CHAPTER 3

FROM DUALISM TO

MATERIALISM

DUALISM

It looks very much as though consciousness is totally different from the physical body. In Chapter 1 we saw that consciousness was in the private domain, non-spatial, non-extended, indivisible and outside the loop of energy transfer whereas the body was part of the public world, spatially located, extended, divisible and involved in the transfer of energy. The conclusion reached by Descartes when he considered the nature of mind and body was that they were two separate substances. By a substance he meant something that could exist independently or without being dependent on anything else. To Descartes it is possible that the mind might exist without the body and that the body might exist without the mind. This position came to be known as substance dualism or, when we mean specifically Descartes' version, Cartesian dualism.

His dualism was controversial even in his own day and has remained so ever since. There was one particular problem that it confronted and to which Descartes gave a less than satisfactory answer. Descartes wanted to hold two beliefs that many other people have regarded as incompatible. On the one hand he asserted, as we have seen, that the mind and the body were quite different in their natures and properties. (Particularly important to Descartes were the ideas of spatiality, extension and divisibility.) On the other hand it seemed to him self-evident that the body affected the mind and that the mind affected the body; in other words that there was interaction between mind and body. Most people would agree with Descartes as regards interaction: it seems obvious that a damaged toe (physical) causes pain (mental) and that intentions (mental) cause bodily actions (physical).

But can there be interaction between mind and body if one is non-physical, non-extended and non-spatial and the other is physical, extended and spatial? It seems difficult, to say the least, to make any sense of a non-physical cause of a physical event and vice versa. (We saw the problem in connection with pain and vision in Chapter 1.) Points like this were put to Descartes who, when pressed, came up with the explanation that there was a part of the body, the pineal gland in the brain (an organ whose function was unknown in his day) where there was contact between the mind and the body. His explanation has not been considered plausible for the following reason: the pineal gland is a physical object as much as any other part of the body. As a physical object it is by definition extended and spatially located. The difficulty of explaining how something that is physical can be in a cause-and-effect relationship with something that is non-physical has not been overcome.

There is no doubt that dualism has an intuitive appeal. It certainly seems to be the case that our minds are nothing like our brains. But in spite of this over the centuries since Cartesian dualism first entered the discourse of philosophers it has been challenged by the interaction problem. Most philosophers agree that you cannot seriously believe in both substance dualism and interaction between mind and body.

One or the other has to be jettisoned. There have been many attempts since Descartes' day to understand what the mind and consciousness are and how they relate to the body. What I want to address next is a theory that is strikingly opposite to dualism. Instead of there being two substances that exist, the mind and the body, might it be that there is just one?

MATERIALISM

Look anywhere in the human body and you will find limbs, organs and so on that are made of cells. Look more deeply into cells and you find that they are complex organisations of chemicals. At a still more fundamental level the components of those chemical are the elements, the building blocks of all matter — no conscious states, no mind revealed under the microscope but just extracts from the elements and compounds of which the earth is composed. In a very popular song of the 1960s was the refrain 'We are stardust', not just a romantic notion but a literal truth in the sense that the elements of which our bodies are composed were forged millions of year ago in the furnaces of stars. Every atom in our body was once part of a star and indeed, before that, arose out of the primordial hydrogen of the early stages of the universe.

Do these facts about the composition of the human body help us resolve some of the problems of an intransigent consciousness encountered earlier? Could we find an answer to all these difficulties with one simple expedient? Why don't we say that it has just been a mistake to think of the conscious mind and the body as completely different from each other? Maybe the truth is that they are one and the same thing. It isn't difficult to see the appeal of this idea, that the mind, including consciousness, is just the physical brain and not something mysteriously separate. And it certainly solves some problems. For, as long as we persist with the position that there are two quite incompatible substances in existence, the physical brain on the one hand and non-physical consciousness on the other, we will be unable to explain convincingly how they can interact, whether it is the brain causing consciousness (the neurons in George's brain affected by his damaged toe causing him pain) or consciousness acting on the brain (the non-physical pain in George's mind making him rub his toe). So, if we simply ditch the idea of dualism, we resolve that problem at a stroke. In fact, we see that it was a pseudo problem all the time.

What we need is a monist theory, that is, a theory that there is a single type of stuff in the universe. We can then apply the principle of Ockham's razor, a very old idea that, put briefly, says that if you can solve a problem in a simple way, why add unnecessary complications? With one substance we won't have any problems whatsoever of interaction. A neat and tidy solution!

What then is this one substance, this one type of stuff? There are two obvious contenders here: the view that everything is somehow mental and the view that everything is somehow physical. Those who believe that the only substance is the mental are usually called idealists: those who believe that the only substance is the physical are usually called materialists (or, as some prefer, physicalists).

It ought to be pointed out at this stage that both terms have a specialised meaning in philosophy which is different from their everyday usage. A philosophical materialist is not someone selfishly obsessed with possessions, with the acquisition of more and more consumer goods but someone who holds the view that everything that exists is ultimately made of matter (or, in a slightly weaker form of materialism) explicable in terms of matter. A philosophical idealist is not someone with unrealistic hopes, with a romantic or quixotic take on life, but someone who holds that all that exists is mental states in minds and that there are no physical objects independent of the mind.

I will postpone a discussion of idealism until a later chapter for two reasons: first, most people when they encounter idealism find it a strange, even weirdly unsettling view; second, idealism is a position held or even taken seriously by very few. By contrast, there are many people both now and in many periods of history who would call themselves materialists.

Three reasons come to mind immediately that make materialism sound a plausible and persuasive explanation. First, the history of the universe, as far as we know it, is a history of purely physical change. From the initial explosive 'big bang' to the formation of hydrogen atoms, the development of stars and the planet earth, through all the stages of the earth's progress: its cooling, the movement of tectonic plates, the flow of glaciers, the rise and fall of mountain ranges, the beginnings of plant life and then of animals, throughout the whole of this process all the events that have occurred have exclusively involved physical objects in a state of flux, i.e., atoms and molecules forming, separating and reforming into a multitudinous range of shapes, whether they be oceans or dragonflies, forests or the intricate pathways of the human brain. And we assume that all the objects involved in this process of non-stop change are without exception physical objects with a spatial location and with measurable dimensions. Against this background it seem sensible, to say the least, to assume that everything that is real is physical. The arrival at some point of a non-physical, non-spatial, non-dimensional consciousness from who knows where now sounds an implausible idea. Why not then assume physical monism as the best explanation?

Second, if we isolate the individual human body from this process, your body or my body, we find another pressing case for keeping exclusively to the physical in our explanations. For we all had our origins in a single cell, a complex piece of biological machinery which divided and divided; other cells took on a range of functions in different parts of the body, including the specialised cells that inhabit the nervous system, the neurons. All totally physical things. We can trace our individual physical origins from a single cell to a foetus to the baby at birth to the toddler and so on to our present bulk gradually built up by the ingestion of substances extracted from food. All physical input. Through our sense organs arrived billions of pieces of data in the form of light waves, sound waves and tiny particles. More physical input. What we are today is the culmination by a step-by-step accretion of a purely physical input, processed by an increasingly complex but purely physical nervous system. Where in all these explicable stages of greater and greater biological complexity is there room or a role for a completely different type of entity? How could a non-physical consciousness have arisen out of a physical body? As you can see again here, materialism has a serious case to make.

Third, the success of scientific studies of the brain has persuaded many people that the best explanation is that mind and consciousness is one and the same as the brain. This approach begins with the notion of correlations. A correlation is a repeated one-to-one relationship between two things. There is a correlation between rising temperatures in summer and increases in ice cream sales, between the rise and fall of tides and the position of the moon, between the imminence of a general election and the degree of charm evident in politicians. Sometimes there is a causal link between the two things in the correlation, in the case of the moon and the tides, for instance. But sometimes the correlation is best explained by the fact that what seemed to be two things in this one-to-one relationship are on closer analysis found to be one and the same thing. There is, for example, a correlation between an object, say a poker held in a fire becoming hotter and the degree to which the molecules of which the poker is made becoming more agitated. Physicists tell us that this correlation is explained by the fact that heat just is one and the same thing as molecular motion.

There are clearly correlations between events taking place in the brain and the conscious states that we experience. To see this point all we need to assume is that the sense organs send information to the brain when there is a conscious experience. My drinking coffee precedes my tasting coffee; similarly in the case of sniffing a sweet pea, touching an ice block: change to brain first, followed by change to conscious state. When I see a tree, my eyes must first have received data from the outside world; when I hear a bell, the sound experience comes after the brain has received the data via the ear and so on. All fairly obvious correlations. (If the information is blocked by an anaesthetic, then there is no conscious state; so the brain must be stimulated before there is a conscious experience.) Here are some other correlations that make the point:

BRAIN EVENT caused by:	CONSCIOUS STATES
damage to tissue, e.g., stubbing a toe	pain
chemicals, e.g., alcohol, LSD	changed conscious states
blow to head	seeing stars, loss of consciousness
infected food	nausea
spinning body	dizziness
staring at a computer screen for many hours	headache
information re approaching large bear	sense of panic, rapid thoughts
reading letter announcing lottery win	sense of surprise and joy

Nowadays in addition to this intuitive case for a correlation we have the very extensive evidence from modern scanners to show that particular areas of the brain are active when we have conscious experiences. Indeed, it may be the case that there is a complete one-to-one correlation between particular brain events, called neural correlates, and accompanying conscious states. This may not be possible to prove at the moment but it makes sense to follow this line as a very plausible explanation. (We will return to this point in Chapter 6.) Materialists take the regular correlation between what is happening in the brain and the conscious state as evidence that the brain and consciousness are the same. We will have to consider next whether they have a good case for this claim.

Materialism is a theory with very ancient origins. We first find it in European philosophy in the work of the Greek thinker, Democritus (c.460 – c.370 BC). He held that everything in the universe was made up of invisible and indivisible units called atoms. In fact, the word 'atomos' in Greek means 'that which cannot be cut or divided'.

He believed that these atoms had always been in existence and could never perish in a universe without beginning or end. Everything in the universe was composed of atoms: stars, planets, rocks, plants, animal and human bodies. Atoms were thought to be in constant motion and over time they came together to form objects like stars, planets and so on which held their shape for a while before disintegrating into the atoms existing separately once again.

Here is an example of the way Democritus might have been thinking. Picture thousands of starlings dotted about the land gathering one day in a V formation as they begin to migrate, holding that shape during the journey and then at the destination one by one moving apart as individual units, the shape lost as each bird goes its own way for the next season. That is what a physical object is like, a temporary collection of a group of atoms. Or think of droplets of water vapour randomly located coming together to form clouds for a few hours and later separating into individual raindrops. Physical objects are transient fusions of atoms. Among these temporary collections of atoms are human bodies. For the implication of materialism for us is that we are no more than chance and temporary bondings of constantly moving physical particles.

This materialist view did not mean that there was not a soul. To Democritus we each indeed had a soul or 'psyche' but it was not in any way non-material. It was composed of atoms just like the body but of a finer structure than those which made up the body. Perception was explained like this. When we had experiences of seeing, hearing, smelling, tasting and touching, what happened was that a film of atoms was emitted from the surface of objects that we were seeing, hearing etc. and interacted with the atoms of the soul. No mystery here of a non-physical consciousness in some kind of relation with the physical but a purely physical process from start to finish. The materialism of Democritus was also explored in the philosophy of Epicurus (341-270 BC) and the poetry of Lucretius (c.99-c.55 BC) in his *De Rerum Natura* (*On the Nature of the Universe*).

After centuries of rejection in Christian philosophy and on the cusp of modern science materialism re-emerged in the work of Thomas Hobbes (1588–1671). Unlike the materialists of the ancient world Hobbes accepted that there was a distinction between conscious beings like men and such unconscious things as stars, planets, stones and trees, holding that there was within us some sort of representation of the world like a brain map or diagram. But to Hobbes this did not mean that there were two types of entities. He did not deny the existence of a mind that thinks and perceives but he did deny that mind was in any way distinct from the body. To him mind was 'nothing but the motions in certain parts of an organic body' reacting to motions from outside, or, as we might say today, to the sensory input from the external world.

According to the materialist theories considered so far, from Democritus to Hobbes, when we have sense experiences there is physical continuity between the input from the external world and the internal reaction of the body. Indeed, since mind is part of the universe which is physical in all respects, the terms 'external' and 'internal' are strictly misnomers. There is no boundary or barrier between the outer world of matter and an inner world of mind. And so there is no mystery of anything non-physical existing outside a chain of physical causes and effects. By contrast dualism, as we have seen, certainly accepts that there are physical events taking place but claims that there exists over and above them the quite distinct phenomenon of consciousness and that it is not reducible to the physical events. You can see how problems become much simpler if there is only one substance.

The French philosopher, La Mettrie (1709-1751) like Hobbes, found no place at all for a non-physical mind in his description of man. He was more concerned than Hobbes, however, to emphasise the purely mechanical nature of the workings of the human body. All human motion and activity to La Mettrie are explicable in terms of natural forces which obey the laws of nature. He explored evidence from the animal world — for example, that a frog's heart moved when extracted from the frog, that a chicken continued to run after it had been decapitated — to show that the idea of a non-physical mind is an unnecessary hypothesis in any explanation of animate behaviour. What are called conscious states are, to La Mettrie, simply part of the cause-and-effect physical system of the human body. 'The brain has its muscles for thinking,' he wrote, 'just as the legs have muscles for walking'. The Italian scientist, Galvani (1737–1798) showed the mechanical nature of animal bodies when he applied an electric current to the leg of a dissected frog and caused it to move, an experiment that was one of the inspirations for Mary Shelley's *Frankenstein*. In that novel Victor Frankenstein collects the body parts of corpses and from them forms a new body. How he brings them to life is left conveniently vague by Mary Shelley. Early film versions implied that he passed an electric current through the limbs and organs and 'galvanised' them into life.

MIND-BRAIN IDENTITY

The modern version of materialism when applied to the problem of the relationship between mind including consciousness and the brain goes under the name of mind-brain identity theory. During the second half of the twentieth century it was developed with considerable sophistication.

These latter-day materialists tried to deal head-on with the fact that the mind-set of most people is in the first instance dualistic; the burden of proof seemed to fall most definitely on them. And we can easily see why. For, in spite of the strong intellectual appeal mentioned earlier of materialism, the idea that the brain is the mind is not one we grasp intuitively. It does not strike us immediately as true like the fact that the shortest distance between two points is a straight line. What we **mean** by the mind is certainly not what we **mean** by the brain. Indeed, it seems absolutely obvious that a sense experience of smelling turpentine or a vivid memory of a sunset during last summer's holiday is anything but the same as a bundle of neurons firing in the brain. Common-sense seems most definitely to be on the side of the dualists in this respect. But modern identity theorists are not put off by common-sense and rightly so. After all, common-sense used to tell us that the sun moved across the sky and that the earth was flat. So how does identity theory overcome the straightforward objection that, since conscious states do not in the slightest resemble the brain, they can hardly be one and the same thing?

Well, they draw a distinction between meaning and reference. We might have two different words with two different meanings but they may refer to the same thing. Suppose George buys a vase for 50p in a car boot sale, places it on his mantelpiece and puts in it a single rose. Unknown to him, his wife, Jane, takes it to the *Antiques Road Show* and finds that it is the uniquely surviving piece from a once famous pottery and made hundreds of years ago for use in royal ceremonies. George and Jane certainly do not mean the same thing when he says 'cheap vase' and she says 'priceless chalice'. But their different names do in fact refer to one and the same thing. So the materialists were on the right lines in affirming that meaning and reference are quite distinct.

Could some such confusion of naming account for our different terms, 'consciousness' and 'brain'? The difference between George and Jane as regards the vessel, perhaps after talking at cross purposes for a while, is easily resolved — they will soon tell that they are looking at the same object — the words 'brain' and 'consciousness', however, present a much more challenging problem.

Take instead an example which fits the materialists' case more effectively. I mentioned clouds and water vapour a moment ago. Now what I mean by water vapour droplets on my car windscreen is quite different from what I mean by a cloud in the sky but it is without doubt the case that a cloud just is water vapour. So the fact that I mean two quite different things by the two terms ('water droplets' and 'cloud') is no argument against them being one and the same thing. Does this example better fit the mind and brain relationship?

There is a problem when we try to apply this example to the case in point. If I doubt whether a cloud is indeed water vapour, then those doubts can be removed. I can look at the drops of water vapour on my car window and walk into a cloud, say, a low-lying cloud sitting on a mountain, and there I can discover for myself that the cloud really is composed of water vapour. And think of the identity of Dr Jekyll and Mr Hyde (or of Superman and Clark Kent). The problem here can be resolved by tracing a line from one person to the other person who is allegedly different and finding that they are one and the same. If you tracked Dr Jekyll twenty-four hours a day, you would discover his common identity with Mr Hyde. Can I trace some sort of line from the brain to the mind and back again? But here is the problem. I don't see how I could make this work. And the reason why rests on two of the crucial differences between the mental and the physical we discussed in Chapters 1 and 2. They are:

a. Since the mind just is not capable of being given a particular location in space, I cannot trace a line from the brain to consciousness in the way that I can trace one between two things that do have a location in space, from water vapour droplets to a cloud. If you start with the brain as Dr Jekyll, how do you find your way to Mr Hyde as consciousness?

b. Whereas the cloud and water vapour share the characteristic of existing in the public domain — they are out there in the external world and open to measurement, the mental is accessed only from the first-person viewpoint. There is no way I can trace a line from the third-person viewpoint to the first-person viewpoint.

But materialists are not going to give up yet. They have more subtle examples to make their case. What about heat? When we say that a poker is hot or cold, we have a precise meaning in mind. When we say that the molecules of the poker are greatly or only very slightly agitated, we mean something very different. But, as we have already seen, physics has taught us that heat just is molecular motion. The molecules of the poker which has been in the fire are much busier, in much more frenzied motion than they were when it lay on the hearth.

This analogy sounds more promising for the mind and body relationship. And its appeal goes further than that. It is an example of the way that scientific understanding has developed over the last few centuries. Science solved the mystery of the nature of heat when it discovered that it was molecular motion. It has solved many more. What is lightning? It turns out that it is an electrical discharge. People will have been aware of lightning for the whole of human history and more recently have learned about electricity. Who would have thought that the two would turn out to be the same? The problem of consciousness — is that next in line to be cleared up by the advance of science when it is discovered that consciousness just is the activity of neurons in the brain? Mankind has always known consciousness; in recent years knowledge of the very minutely detailed operations of the brain has greatly expanded. Could consciousness be the next mystery to succumb to the advances of science?

OBJECTIONS

1. THE MEAT OBJECTION

I mentioned earlier that the idea that consciousness was one and the same thing as the brain was counterintuitive. That is putting it mildly. Just consider for a moment what the brain actually is.

It is, obviously, a part of the body; it is made of cells like the rest of the body , though it contains a particular sort of cell called the neuron. Now if the brain is consciousness as well as being a collection of cells what reason is there for these cells and only these cells having the amazing extra ability to double as conscious states? Liver cells don't do it; neither do heart, kidney, lung and pancreas cells. So what is so special about the cells found in the brain that makes them have consciousness as well as being physical objects? Is there some feature of brain cells that is not present in other sorts of cells that might give a clue? If we were to examine under a microscope both neurons and, say, cells from the heart, would we be able to detect some significant difference between them, a difference that makes one type bearers of experience, of sounds and smells and thoughts and so on, and the other one just cells with a bodily functions? I don't think so.

Well, there is a physical difference between neurons and other cells in the body. All cells respond to chemical signals and in the case of all cells there is a difference between the electrical charge inside them and outside them. What distinguishes a neuron from other cells is that the neuron has a complicated communication system built into it: branch-like dendrites (from *dendron*, Greek for tree) receiving information and one tentacle-like axon sending information outwards. But, however more complex the neuron is in comparison with other cells, it remains a collection of molecules operating as a biological mechanism.

Let me put the point even more bluntly. The brain is part of the meat of the body. (This comparison is not original. You will find it in *The Mysterious Flame* by Colin McGinn who himself links the idea to a science fiction story by Terry Bisson.) Quite literally. We think animals have conscious states. Certainly, the more complex animals like cows and pigs. Well, the brains of both animals are treated as meat and form part of the cuisine of some cultures. It didn't take me long to find a recipe for cow brain (Cajun fried brain) and pig brain (a Filipino dish *tortang utak* or pig's brain omelette). And we don't need to explore cannibalism to see the implications for the human brain. Brains are part of the too, too solid, fleshy, meaty, one hundred per cent physicality of the human body. And yet according to mind-brain identity theory they are supposed to be one and the same as the experience of adding up a sum, of hearing lilting melodies and having a surge of compassion. How could this be?

2. THE MARMITE OBJECTION

According to its label Marmite contains: yeast extract, salt, vegetable extract, niacin, thiamin, spice extracts, riboflavin, folic acid, celery extract and vitamin B12. It is possible to analyse items on that list in more depth; salt is sodium chloride, riboflavin is a B vitamin and so on. We could continue the breakdown by analysing sodium and chloride and by breaking riboflavin down to its basic chemistry. An expert in food science might know all the available information about the chemical structure of Marmite.

When George enjoys eating a Marmite sandwich, the Marmite makes contact with taste buds on his tongue. The tongue has a specialized area for each of the four basic tastes: sweet, sour, salt, bitter. Taste buds are 20 to 40 millionths of an inch wide and contain 30 to 80 receptors which send information via cranial nerves to the brain. This is a totally physical process, out in the open, measurable, public. Again an expert might know all the available information about how the taste buds work, how they send information to the brain and how the brain processes that information.

Suppose Jane becomes that expert: she studies both the food science of Marmite and the physiology of taste and knows all that there is to know about what happens when Marmite makes contact with taste buds and sends information to the brain. And suppose also that Jane has never actually tasted Marmite. Would she on the basis of all the information she has acquired be able to predict what the taste of Marmite is like?

Now Jane might assume that because Marmite contains salt it is likely to taste salty. But she only knows what salty foods taste like because she has tasted them in the past. If we go back a stage and she had never tasted any salty food but was given all the information about what salt is composed of and how the brain processes the data etc., she would find herself in exactly the same situation as she is now in with regard to Marmite.

So would she be able to predict the taste of Marmite? The answer is surely no. She would not know the quality of the taste of Marmite from all her knowledge, however extensive and detailed it has become. Is this because there is still some information missing about the chemical make up of Marmite or about how the taste system works in the brain? Imagine, then, that in the future vast sums of money over many years are invested in the chemistry of Marmite and the study of the taste system and there are major additions to the sum of knowledge. Would the future even more knowledgeable Jane be in a better position to know, in advance of tasting, what the flavour of Marmite is like?

I see no reason to think that she would. The special and distinctive quality of the taste is not included in the list of physical ingredients. The sense experience of the taste somehow exists over and above the facts of chemistry and brain systems.

The taste of Marmite is a conscious experience. If mind-brain identity theory is right, then it is identical with the brain. Let me be more precise here. When George is tasting Marmite, his brain is in a particular state. A certain number of his one hundred billion neurons are active at that time. Identity theory is committed to the view that the brain in this particular condition just is the same thing as that taste of Marmite. And yet all this knowledge gives us not the slightest inkling about what it is like actually to taste Marmite. At the very least this conclusion makes it difficult to maintain the position that consciousness and the brain are one and the same thing.

3. THE PROBLEM OF NARROW DEFINITIONS

George is hearing thunder. If the mind-brain identity theory is correct, then that hearing experience is one and the same as the particular state his brain is in at this time. Let us assume that for any hearing experience, a particular type of conscious state, is identical with a particular type of brain state and look at some of the implications of this view. At the risk of oversimplifying the description of the brain I am taking for granted that certain neurons in a particular area of his brain are active when George hears something like thunder and I am going to call the activity of these neurons this area, H Activity.

Assuming identity theory, then we can affirm that if there is H Activity, then there must be hearing going on; conversely, if there is hearing going on, there must be H Activity. It is like saying that when Superman is rescuing humanity, then Clark Kent must be rescuing humanity or that when Clark Kent is typing an article, then Superman must be typing an article. These conclusions are bound to follow from the fact that Superman and Clark Kent are one and the same person. The same applies in the case of hearing experiences and H Activity in the brain.

Now thunder is very loud. If you can hear anything you can hear thunder and, as a thought experiment to test identity theory, I am going to imagine that also in the range of the thunder are the following: several other people, a dog, an octopus and a visitor from a distant planet. When unexpectedly there is a very loud thunderclap, all present react: a sudden start, a yelp, a twitch or whatever. This may sound cruel but I am now going to take all present to a medical laboratory to conduct an experiment. They are put one by one into a scanning device so that their brains can be examined as they are hearing a loud sound like thunder. Later I look at the results. Surprisingly, in none of them is found evidence of H Activity. In the brains of people who can hear perfectly well and answer my questions about hearing the thunder sound, other parts of the brain fire when they hear sounds but that particular H Activity is not found; in the dog, and especially in the octopus, there are also other areas of their neurons that deal with sound information even more remote from the H Activity found in George than in the people. In the case of the extra-terrestrial visitor there is not a single neuron at all; he can certainly hear as I can easily test and he has a brain of sorts but it is nothing like the human brain being made of what looks like a non-biological material bearing no resemblance to the living cells of the human or animal brain.

These findings present a problem for identity theorists with their belief that a particular type of conscious state, in this case of hearing, is identical with a particular type of brain state, in this case H Activity. There is no H Activity in the other subjects and yet they appear to be able to hear just as much as George appears to be able to hear. But if identity theory is true, without H Activity there just cannot be any hearing. How can this be? We are left with two options: either

a. only George and people with similar brains are having hearing experiences; the others show hearing behaviour but they lack conscious awareness of sound

or

b. hearing experiences are not one and the same as H Activity.

Option a) seems ridiculously exclusive and illustrates dramatically the problem of narrowness. Identifying consciousness with a particular type of brain is just too narrow a definition to work. Are we really going to say that only where we find H Activity there is consciousness of hearing? If we persisted in this view, we would be ascribing to vast swathes of animals and, perhaps, to many of our fellow humans a great void in consciousness, a complete deafness to the sounds of babies crying, to bird song and earthquake rumbles and giving arbitrarily to George and his brain-state doubles a special privilege purely on the grounds that they share a particular brain structure and configuration.

It is interesting to note some other implications. You may or may not believe that there exist a God and angels. But if they do exist it is difficult to see how identity theory could allow that they could have conscious experiences. And the idea of God or of an angel not being conscious makes no sense at all. Whatever may be the answer to such difficult theological questions as whether God has a body or what sort of bodies, if any, angels have, I don't think that anyone proposes that they have brains like human ones. The idea of humanity being made in the image of God cannot surely be that literal, can it? But, as we have seen, identity theory requires brains of a very particular sort and in very particular conditions for consciousness.

Water is one and the same thing as H_2O. Anything that is water is H_2O and anything that is H_2O is water. Similarly a particular type of conscious state is a particular type of brain state and any particular type of brain state is a particular type of conscious state. Just as a liquid that is not H_2O is not water, so a being that lacks the right sort of brain and the right sort of activity is not conscious. It follows that God, angels, humans with different brain configurations, animals without H Activity and possible beings with brains made of non-biological material cannot be conscious. Can we avoid this conclusion? If consciousness is indeed one and the same thing as a particular brain state, that is where this narrow theory of identity leads.

4. THE PROBLEM OF WIDE DEFINITIONS

Could the mind be made of blancmange, of seaweed, of candyfloss? What an absurd suggestion.

We have got used to the idea of the mind being closely related to the brain. And there can be no closer relationship than the two being one and the same, in other words, identity. But when we come to think afresh of the idea of the brain as the mind and consciousness, that is, without the influence of years and years of familiarity, when we look at it as though it were a new idea just presented to us cold today, then it seems very odd that anyone should come to think in the first place that the collection of communication cells in the squishy walnut shaped filler of the skull, should be the same thing as our rushes of passion, our panicky fears, our bright and less bright ideas, the taste of gorgonzola and the sound of alarm clocks. But somehow we have been persuaded, at least many people have been persuaded, that the brain is consciousness.

What we were considering in Section 3 of this chapter is often called 'type identity' theory. Although the problems we have met are very damaging to the idea of mind-brain identity, it need not mean that we have to dismiss completely the view that the best answer to the question what is consciousness is that it is material substance in some sense. The claim has been that a certain type of conscious state is just one and the same thing as a certain type of physical state. I made up the example of hearing as H Activity. An example often used is that pain is one and the same as c-fibres firing. We looked at pain in Chapter 1.

Now suppose we drop the requirement of one type being the same as another type. What I mean is that instead of saying that this type of conscious state is the same as this type of brain condition, we loosen up the identity idea by simple asserting that any conscious state is a physical state of some sort. This change would allow that a conscious experience of hearing or of pain might be one type of physical state in some humans, another in other humans, and different again in animals and in potential extra-terrestrial travellers. So hearing is H Activity in George and people like him, K Activity in people with different brain configurations; in animals it might be a quite different cluster of cells but still biological and in the alien visitor some non-biological system of engineering.

In this way we get rid of another implausible conclusion. Consider this: if type identity theory really worked, it would be possible to discover whether a being, human animal or whatever was conscious purely by looking in its brain to see if it had particular characteristics. It is quite conceivable that we might find H Activity or c-fibres firing in a being we had no other reason whatsoever to believe was conscious. (The more you look at the implications the stranger type identity theory becomes.)

According to this adaptation of the concept of identity, however, we no longer draw a boundary around the particular characteristics of the human brain and say whatever is outside this boundary does not have conscious experiences. So what is now allowed to be identical with consciousness? If a being showed all the symptoms in behaviour of having pains, of being able to hear and so on and if, when its brain was scanned, it turned out to be made of electrical wiring, would we allow that it had conscious experiences? And why stop at electrical wiring? What about a brain made of string, of twigs, of seaweed, of blancmange? You see the problem now is quite the opposite. Before (in Section 3) we had only one thing to consider as the brain and consciousness; that was a much too narrow definition. Now there doesn't seem to be any way of excluding any type of material whatsoever as capable of being not just the seat of consciousness but consciousness itself. We have the opposite problem: the definition is too wide and inclusive to be of much help to our understanding. We have veered too far in the opposite direction and maybe now we have too few limits. It looks as though just about anything could be consciousness.

CHAPTER FOUR

MATERIALISM REVISITED

FUNCTIONALISM

In this examination of identity theory it has proved very difficult to pin down the particular nature of the physical stuff that constitutes consciousness. In view of this difficulty why not try another direction?

Some things we define not in terms of a description of what they are but of a description of what they do. Take a word like poison. What we mean by 'poison' is a substance taken into the body and causing death or serious illness. The definition of poison, then, is not expressed in terms of what poison is made of but in terms of what poison does. Many different things can be poisons and we do not need to know precisely what they are to use the term 'poison' very effectively. Some examples of poisons are: hemlock, strychnine, arsenic, carbon monoxide, cyanide, lead, mercury, botulin, a bite from certain types of snake, paraquat, polonium — all very different types of substances. A law of the land could very effectively decree that the administering of poison to a person constitutes a serious crime. It does not need to specify in detail what poisons are made of. In fact, it would be much better if it did not since the law would already be in place to include any new substance that might be used with a similarly harmful effect. (If an act of Parliament made in the middle of the nineteenth century had outlawed killing by poison, no one could have included polonium on a list of poisons. It was only discovered in 1898 but it was used in a notorious murder in London in 2007.)

We have encountered the problem (the blancmange brain problem) that makes it very difficult to say what type of thing consciousness is and what it is not in Chapter 3. So, taking a hint from the poison example let us see if we can define consciousness not in terms of what it is but in terms of what it does. As we did in Chapter 1, we can start with pains as a striking example of consciousness.

George stubs his toe against the bathroom door; he winces, yells, rubs his toe. In between those two events is the pain. Not knowing what the pain is for reasons explained earlier, we define pain in terms of what it does. Pain is both

   a. that which is caused by damage to the body, for example, stubbing a toe

   and also

   b. the cause of certain types of behaviour like wincing, yelling out, rubbing the toe.

This approach to an explanation of consciousness is called functionalism. It really does not matter much to the functionalists what pain is any more than it matters to lawmakers what type of poison is used in a crime. Pain is the intermediary between damage to body tissue and pain behaviour (toe rubbing for George). This view also has an advantage over behaviourism. One problem with behaviourism was that it identified pain with behaviour, wincing, crying ouch and so on and that seemed intuitively wrong. For we easily distinguish between the cause of the behaviour and the behaviour itself. Functionalism allows us to do just that.

So much for functionalism and pain. What about other types of conscious experience?

It is straightforward to fit other examples of conscious experience into a functionalist framework. Look at the following:

STAGE 1: INPUT	STAGE 2: MIND	STAGE 3: OUTPUT
sound waves from alarm clock	waking up experience	bodily movement
reading a letter bringing bad news	sadness	weeping
stubbing a toe	pain	rubbing the toe
abusive language	anger	anger behaviour, e.g. fist clenching

But there are several reasons for resisting functionalism that need to be explored. A couple of them we have met before in the analysis of identity theory. The problem with functionalism, as we can see, is that it does not really address consciousness head on. First, Jane has no way of ascertaining from observing George whether he has the same quality of experience that she has. At the concert both are having the same sound input and both may be smiling with apparent satisfaction but is her hearing-the-oboe experience the same as his? It certainly might be but it equally might not be. In a functionalist assessment of the situation, however, it would make no difference whether it was or not. Second, briefly back to the zombie problem, since we only observe Stage 1 and Stage 3 in other people, it is perfectly possible that they do not have Stage 2. If Jane sees George stub his toe and then a moment later rub his toe, her observation is exactly the same whether or not George undergoes the experience of pain: a conscious George and a zombie George are indistinguishable to Jane.

But there is an even more fundamental point that was mentioned in the Introduction. Contemporary attempts to make sense of consciousness usually begin with the assumption that the physical is not a problem: the problem is fitting consciousness into a framework which is physical. What is the place of consciousness in nature, the physical world, is the question posed time after time. Functionalism is part of that general approach. With the history of mind-brain identity to act as a warning functionalists abandon the attempt to give a description of consciousness and approach it in a more indirect way.

But it seems very odd to me to address the problem from that starting point. For consciousness is surely what we are certain of first and foremost. It is consciousness then, surely, not the physical that should be our first base. We know conscious experiences at first hand without any intermediary; the physical world we know via the conscious experience. Consider this last point in more detail. My knowledge of trees and doors, of houses and other people is not direct. It is the seeing or hearing or whatever sense experience it happens to be that is direct and known. Sense experience is the basis of everything we claim to know about the material world. And yet functionalists set out to present it and consciousness in general as some secondary kind of phenomenon, an anomaly to be fitted into an otherwise seamless understanding of reality.

OBJECTIONS TO FUNCTIONALISM
CAUSE AND EFFECT

Functionalism regards conscious states as effects of physical causes. The damage to the toe is the cause of whatever the pain is. It also regards the pain as itself a cause, that is, of the physical reaction, the movement of rubbing the toe. But let me concentrate here just on the idea that the body is the cause of the conscious state. One sort of causation is enough to be going on with for the moment.

We mean different things by the term 'cause'. Sometimes we mean that to cause is to make or construct or form something new. For example, when we take a cake out of the oven, we consider the cake to be the end result caused by the assembling and mixing of the ingredients and the heat of the oven and so on. The cake was caused to be by all that process. We can trace the changes made to the ingredients and see how the soft texture and sponginess of the cake arose out of the ingredients and what was done to them. But causing obviously does not always involve a process of making. A bad tyre causes an accident; a dropped cigarette causes a fire. These are examples of a different sense of cause.

If we consider that brain events could be the cause of conscious experience, we need to clarify what sense of causation we are dealing with. There are problems with both senses of cause and effect in the examples above when we try to apply them to the case of the brain allegedly causing consciousness.

Take the cake example. We start with ingredients that can be weighed and measured, the flour, the margarine and so on and we end with something that can be weighed and measured, the cake. And we also have good reason to believe that no energy was either gained or lost during the cooking process.

When we look at the brain and consciousness, however, we may begin with the measurable ingredients, the particular set of neurons firing in the brain but we end with non-spatial, non-dimensional experiences. And in contravention of the law of conservation and mass we seem to have gained something without the expenditure of any energy (a problem we met in Chapter 1). So it does not seem that we can understand the idea of the brain as the cause of consciousness using this analogy.

In the case of causal events like the faulty tyre and the accident, the dropped cigarette and the fire, a key feature is that a chain of physical contact can be traced. When a tyre with insufficient grip is turned and fails to gain purchase, the momentum of the car drives it towards another car. All through the process there is what is called contiguity; cause and effect works when one thing is in direct contact with, is actually touching something else (contiguous means next to or touching). There aren't any gaps in the causal process. Similarly, in the case of the cigarette: the still burning stub has to touch the carpet for there to be a fire. There are exceptions such as the power of gravity — the moon's effect on tides, for example — but they don't seem apply very closely to the problem of relating consciousness to the brain.

Again it is difficult to see how the idea of the brain causing conscious states could be likened to that sort of process. I won't repeat here the points made in Chapter 2, but we have good reason to reject the idea that a conscious state could be said to be next to or to be touching a brain state. The idea of contiguity is not going to apply.

So what sense could we make of the idea of the brain causing conscious states? Take a radio as an example. There is a completely regular correlation between the position of the volume dial and the decibel level of sound I hear. I suggest that this is also true of the brain and consciousness. Whenever there is firing of this sort in this part of the brain, then there is a particular conscious experience. We can use the C-fibres firing and pain as one example here. Another is a correlation between stimulus to the visual cortex and seeing.

But the dials and the radio do not create the sound that I hear. There is causation in the sense that moving the dials determines what type of sound I hear, music or discussion, but the radio does not make the sound in the sense that the ingredients with their various chemical properties, the cook and the oven make the cake; nor does the radio cause the sound in the way that the faulty tyre caused the accident. The implication of this alternative view of causation is that in some way the sound is already out there available to be tapped by radio. Could this be true of consciousness? (I will return to the analogy with the radio in Chapter 7.)

THE BRAIN, A BRIEF DIGRESSION

The human brain is a physical object. It has a weight of about 1.3 kilograms on average and a size: it is small enough to rest on an open hand. It has a pinky, creamy colour and the consistency of thick blancmange. It is the most complex object known to exist in the universe, containing about a hundred billion specialised cells called neurons. Each neuron may communicate with many thousands and even several hundred thousands of other neurons. Estimates put the number of connections between neurons at one thousand trillion (a trillion is one million million).

The brain is part of the nervous system which can be likened to a network of roads within the body. For example, one set of highways, the peripheral nervous system, relays information from the sense organs to the central nervous system, the brain and the spinal cord. So when someone stubs a toe, a signal is sent from the toe along the nerves to the brain. Information from the face bypasses the spinal cord and goes straight to the brain along what are called cranial nerves.

The brain via this transport system also sends information out to different parts of the body. So there are journeys taking place all the time to and from the brain along the motorways, the A and B roads and the minor lanes and footpaths of the nervous system. The brain receiving and processing information from the input systems controls such bodily functions as heart rate, blood sugar levels, digestion, breathing and blood flow. It also controls the movements of the body, arms, legs, neck, the fingers, for example, of which we are conscious.

Neurons are also physical objects. Their function is to convey messages around the nervous system both within the brain and to and from the brain. Like other cells in the body they contain a nucleus but unlike other cells they have dendrites and an axon. A neuron has many dendrites which are like threads or branches bringing messages into the neuron and a single axon, a long cable or arm whose job is to take messages away from the neuron; the axon itself divides into branches. Communication in the nervous system uses two methods: electrical and chemical. Within the neuron an electrical charge flows up the dendrites to the cell body where it fires and sends a wave of electrical charge down the axon. Communication over a tiny gap between neurons takes place at the synapses which are bulb like in shape and located at the end of the axon. Transmission between neurons at the synapse is a chemical process.

Could this stunningly complicated piece of biological machinery, this network of communication systems with its chemical processes and electrical discharges be one and the same as our consciousness, our feelings of pain, our experiences of hearing, tasting, touching, seeing, smelling, our joys and sorrows, our thoughts, ideas, memories? Could it be the cause of them?

If the attempts to show that consciousness is the brain have failed to be convincing so far, it may be because the approaches have not been sufficiently sophisticated. Let me restate the problem and then present a more subtle response to it.

RAQUEL WELCH AND GOTTFRIED WILHELM LEIBNIZ

In a 1966 film, *Fantastic Voyage*, a submarine and its crew, including the film's stars, Raquel Welch and Stephen Boyd, were shrunk to microscopic size and sent inside a human body. They become small enough to float in the blood stream and travel round the organs of the body.

Imagine reducing the size of the submarine even more and directing it into George's brain. The submarine makes its way among the sections of the brain, visits the amygdala, docks at the hippocampus; the submariners go sightseeing in the visual cortex, sail by any of the billions of neurons, pass through the narrow channels of the synapses. They can observe, take readings and measurements and, like astronauts climbing out of their spaceship on the moon, they leave the submarine to make an even closer examination of their surroundings.

The question is this: will the crew of the submarine in the course of their investigations be able to detect any evidence of consciousness or even a single conscious state?

It is difficult to envisage how they could do this or to make any sense of the idea of finding in all this mass of chemicals fizzing with electrical activity the slightest trace of consciousness. What would it look like? How would they detect it?

Three hundred years before *Fantastic Voyage* was made the German philosopher, Gottfried Wilhelm Leibniz asked much the same question. But in his case instead of reducing human beings to miniature explorers, in his imagination he expanded the size of the brain so that humans of conventional size could roam around inside it. He saw the brain as a great machine or mill with metal components, cogs, wheels, pulleys, chains all busily in motion.

But Leibniz' concern was much the same. It makes no difference whether you imagine the brain blown up in size or imagine a visitor to the brain in miniature. Where in all this moving mechanism was the mind and consciousness? Where amongst the metal cogs were the experiences of the senses, the emotions, the memories?

We are not going to find and no surgeon operating on the brain is ever going to find conscious states within the brain; they just are not things like neurons and blood. They are not objects within the brain.

SUPERVENIENCE

George has downloaded on to his lap top Leonardo da Vinci's Mona Lisa, she of the enigmatic smile. He has decided that he will give the face a more distinctive expression. George does not like ambivalence. For him the woman ought to be either happy or sad. He has invested in software which will allow him to manipulate screen images. He enlarges the picture until the Mona Lisa's lips fill the screen. Now he sets to work to turn the expression first into a wide grin and then into a petulant pout. He can only do this by working at the level of the pixels, the many tiny squares of which his screen is composed. When he has enlarged the images by many magnitudes, he no longer has in front of him a facial expression of any sort but instead a collection of coloured squares. For when magnified many times there is no smile, whether enigmatic or of any other quality, visible on the screen. George sets to work and produces two, in his view, improved versions of da Vinci's masterpiece.

The facial expression, whether enigmatic smile, broad grin or pout, is only a feature of the picture when seen on the large scale. At the level of individual pixels it has disappeared. George's experience with the computerised picture can be an analogy for our problem, the relationship of the mind and consciousness to the brain. The idea is this. Of course, it will never be possible to find conscious states when surgeons are examining the brain at the level of the fine detail or by scanning for neuron activity. Consciousness is not that sort of thing. Just as the smile is a feature of the picture seen as a whole and not at all evident at the level of pixels, maybe consciousness should be regarded as a feature of the brain as a whole rather than at the level of individual neurons.

We can distinguish between the large scale (or the more technical term 'macro' level) and the small scale (or 'micro') level. The claim is that conscious states are not micro but macro features of the brain. When you start to think of the general principle involved it is quite familiar. Take any ordinary solid physical object like a pen. Each atom of which it is made is almost a completely hollow void. The nucleus is an infinitesimally small centrepiece like a football in an empty stadium half a mile across. But a pen, nevertheless, looks solid and certainly feels solid. How can this be? Solidity is a feature of the macro object, the billions and billions of atoms that form the pen; there is no solidity at the level of the individual atoms.

Could this be a clue to the brain and consciousness problem? I need to look at the analogy a little more closely. George can click on the screen and increase or decrease magnitude very easily: one click, the pixels are brought up and enlarged; another click, the whole picture appears of the full facial expression. Imagine a super microscope examining the pen, one so finely tuned that it can even reveal the inside of the atom and put the image on George's screen. One click and he sees an empty screen showing the inner void of the atom containing a tiny dot of the nucleus; another click he sees the whole pen. Micro to macro at the press of a finger. Now we put brain images on the screen. One moment we are looking on the micro scale: cells appear, then molecules, then atoms, the next we are looking at — well, what are we seeing now? For if the analogy were to work, then, just as at the macro scale, we observed the solid pen (or the Mona Lisa's facial expression), so at this level we should observe the conscious states. But we don't. We see the large scale brain. We ought along the lines of the analogies to be coming across consciousness. But that never happens. In fact, we have not found a very good match between macro and micro in the examples and macro and micro in the case of the brain and consciousness.

So the analogy does not really stand up to close examination. And the reason goes back to a topic discussed in Chapter 2. In the examples, at both levels, micro and macro, the objects are in the public domain: the pixels and the facial expression are on George's screen and so are the two views of the pen, at the atomic level and the whole pen version. In the case of the brain and consciousness there is no way of overcoming the fact that, although the brain, like the examples above, is a public object, consciousness is resolutely private and resists any attempt to drag it into the open.

COMPLEXITY AND THE GALAXY

Let us try another tack. Some people have sought an explanation for consciousness in the idea of complexity. Animals and humans are the most complex objects in the universe. The human brain wins the prize for having the greatest complexity of any known object. According to the history of the universe as it is now understood, in the early stages the objects within it were comparatively simple in their make up. At the beginning was the simplest of elements, hydrogen; then came helium and so on. In the stars were formed many of the other elements which we now find on the earth. Plant life was a step up in complexity and with animal and human life were formed fine and intricate connections between nerve cells which gave them, in comparison with the state of the universe at its beginning, a bewilderingly labyrinthine complexity. This increase in complexity coincided, it seems, with the arising of conscious states. Unless we allow that plants and trees have experiences, then in the history of the cosmos consciousness comes into play with the arrival of animals with nervous systems. And as those nervous systems have become more and more complex, culminating for the moment in the human brain of one hundred billion neurons, it seems reasonable to assume that complexity, at the very least, has something to do with consciousness.

Could it be that a being has conscious states simply by virtue of being very complex in its physical construction? In short, is complexity the answer? Does complexity confer consciousness?

Consider the following analogy. In a galaxy there are a hundred billion stars. About the same number of stars in the galaxy, then, as there are neurons in the brain. Imagine that within a galaxy communication pathways are constructed among the stars. Each star is linked to thousands or millions of others in this vastly complex, interlocking system just as in the brain synapses link neurons to thousands or millions of other nerves in a network of connections.

In the case of the very complex brain there are conscious states. The galactic system that we have just turned into a gigantic ganglion of interconnections is now as complex as the brain. It just happens to be built on a much bigger scale. Do we think that it is likely that this galaxy is now conscious? But, if consciousness came about purely by virtue of physical complexity, then surely it must be? But my intuition, at least, is that there is no reason to believe that the galaxy is conscious. In the case of the galaxy we have complexity writ large. But if complexity alone were the reason for consciousness, then we would expect the galaxy to have pains, emotions, sense experiences, ideas, memories and so on. Or perhaps a galactic variation on these themes.

There is no reason to think that size is an inhibiting factor. If complexity is the key requirement for consciousness, then why should there be any difference whether the parts of the ganglion of interconnections are the size of neurons, the size of stars or, for that matter at the other extreme of size, of sub-atomic particles?

Complexity on its own does not seem to offer an explanation of consciousness.

CHAPTER 5

CONSCIOUSNESS FIRST

'I regard consciousness as fundamental. I regard matter as derivative from consciousness. We cannot get behind consciousness. Everything that we talk about, everything that we regard as existing, postulates consciousness.'[2]

Max Planck, physicist (1858-1941)

THE GIVEN

In any inquiry, whether philosophical or of any other sort, a background set of assumptions needs to be in place before a beginning can be made. Historians take for granted that there is a past of events — battles, treaties, coronations — to be investigated, geographers that there is a world of rocks, clouds and oceans to be studied, politicians that there are laws that can be changed and so on. Imagine a conference of geographers having a debate on whether mountains and rivers are real! Such questions are for philosophers not geographers. We can call this network of assumed and agreed beliefs, what we take for granted as the agreed starting point, the 'given' of any subject that is being explored. Philosophy is no different: even the subject in which nothing is supposedly taken for granted and everything is open to question cannot avoid this requirement. It too has its 'given' beliefs.

It is tempting to think otherwise, to believe that it is possible to seek knowledge completely free of any beliefs,

---

2   *The Observer* (January 25th, 1931)

prejudices, inclinations that are built into our system of thought. But it is not realistic to assume that we can attain to these heights of objectivity and look on reality from what amounts to no viewpoint at all, to see with God's eye, as it were. For even if I attempt to sweep away all assumptions I hold at the moment and vow to question everything, taking not a single belief for granted, I will not be able even to begin the task without some presuppositions seeping through the cracks of my resistance. For whatever notion or proposition I might subject first to questioning, to ask of it 'Is it true or is it false?', I must have a standard of truth and falsity that is already in place, an up-and-running set of criteria. And if I start to justify this standard of truth and falsity, I will either throw up my arms in despair at the impossibility of completing the task or embark on an infinite regress of standard after standard. I cannot keep the surrounding sea of beliefs out of my little philosophical boat; in fact, the best I can hope to do is to keep baling out the water as soon as I feel it lapping around my feet.

Although we cannot eradicate all presuppositions, whenever we find ourselves taking for granted any belief that is not a first-order belief, that is to say, whenever we are making an assertion whose justification can be called into question, then we should stop at that point and subject it to rigorous questioning. This is what I mean by baling out the water.

You might find that a political dispute between groups of people centres on the idea of freedom, an ideal agreed by both sides. That freedom is a desirable goal is the given of their debate. However, it may be possible to enquire into what deeper assumptions underpin this idea and to discover

78

that there are more fundamental beliefs on which the idea of freedom is founded. As a consequence what seemed to be the given was in fact an assumption open to more questioning; it was not a foundational idea itself but was supported by beliefs at a more basic level.

So far in this attempt to make sense of consciousness I have by and large adopted the physical-first approach. I have assumed that the physical universe is the given for this enquiry, the starting point where we are dealing with facts that can be safely taken for granted; against this background I have been seeking a place, an explanation for consciousness. But I have not found a convincing answer. Consciousness has remained elusively resistant to this line of enquiry. Maybe the problem is that the physical has been wrongly identified as the given; maybe it is possible to delve below it and find, as in the case of freedom, that it is supported by a layer below it

Suppose then I do some digging around the base of the physical to find out if indeed it is fundamental or exists at a secondary level held up by one below it. Archaeologists at the site of Troy, I understand, have found several layers of remains, each one corresponding with a city built on the ruins of one which predated it. They are naturally keen to find evidence of the first city, the baseline of their excavation. I intend now to scrape away with my philosophical trowel and see what emerges.

A genuinely new idea is rare. It is not surprising to find that philosophical archaeologists have worked on this site before. Some have reached the conclusion that the physical is not the foundation but rests on a deeper layer of substance. In this tradition a major figure was the French philosopher, René Descartes (1596-1650).

DESCARTES

Descartes in his search for a secure foundation of knowledge set out to reject all beliefs which were not indubitable, that is to say, those which were not certain beyond any doubt. In a sense he was trying achieve what I implied a moment ago was beyond our human capacity, to transcend all assumptions believed to be the given and to reach the raw condition of unmediated reality. In his personal quest for knowledge he passed through several stages of scepticism: he found the senses unreliable and so unfit to form the basis of knowledge; he wondered whether, if he could not easily distinguish between being awake and being in a dream, he could claim to know anything about the world around him; and, finally, he introduced the thought experiment of the 'evil demon', a device that enabled him to explore the very disturbing idea that all his experiences might have been planted in his mind by a malicious being intent on a wholesale deceit.

It might be worthwhile to dwell for a moment on this very sceptical point that he had reached in his enquiry. He lived in an age of heated controversies which centred on competing authorities for knowledge. Was knowledge whatever was revealed by scripture and the body of its interpretation developed over centuries by the church? Or was knowledge acquired by the painstaking assembling of observation of the natural world by the empirical methods of science? In his own lifetime the confrontation between Galileo and the Roman Catholic church as regards the relative positions of the earth and the sun had epitomised the more general conflict between these rival claims to authority in knowledge. To some of his contemporaries the attempt on which Descartes had embarked to build a free standing edifice of knowledge was doomed by the relentlessly undermining sabotage of scepticism. To them there was no way of achieving knowledge, full stop. They were global sceptics rejecting all claims by all people from whatever quarter that there was knowledge of any kind. Descartes, however, reached a different conclusion.

After a moment of his own despairing that scepticism might be total, that there was no sound foundation for knowledge whatsoever, he awakened to the revelation that even if there were an 'evil demon' at work and even if everything he had hitherto believed were false, he could now be absolutely certain of one truth at least, the truth that he himself must exist. For even if indeed he were living a lie in every sense, there must be a self, a person, a holder of beliefs to be the victim of this all-consuming deceit. In short, he reasoned from the very fact that there were thoughts, however mistaken they might be, that he must exist (the famous 'cogito ergo sum').

But what was he? Not a flesh and blood human body. For even his own body of head, torso, arms and legs might be a fiction created in the mind by the 'evil demon'. No, first and foremost, he was a conscious, thinking being. To Descartes the first certainty was the existence of conscious states; by contrast, the physical world, including even his own body, needed to be proved; its existence was not self-evident but required demonstration in argument. To Descartes the conscious state of thinking was the first certainty, the foundation on which the structure of knowledge might be built. The physical world, if it was to be known at all, was known not directly but only by inference from the conscious state of thinking. It was this conscious state of thinking that was now revealed to be the given or the foundation.

Descartes is famously a dualist. He believed that there were two substances that could exist independently of each other: the mental and the physical. Remember that, at least to his own satisfaction, he now had found his 'given'. He was absolutely convinced that he existed and that he was first and foremost a thinking being. How was he to reach the conclusion that matter also existed? At the risk of mixing metaphors I think Descartes was trying to achieve two things here: first, he had a foundation of knowledge, of the self as a thinking being on which he hoped to build a structure of certain knowledge; second, he was trying to construct a bridge. A foundation and a bridge? Imagine you are on a journey and arrive at a river. You can see a vague outline in the mist of an opposite bank. There is no chance of swimming across for the water is full of piranhas and crocodiles. So you dig deep on your side, the side you are quite sure of and build a tower; then you try to span the river with a bridge extending from and secured by the tower. Eventually you find solid earth on the other side; you build another tower there; your bridge is complete. At least that is your hope.

Descartes proceeded to build his bridge from knowledge of his own mind and consciousness to knowledge of the external world (or, as we might say, from first-person to third-person knowledge). For Descartes the bridge was God. The stones of its construction were the proofs he presented to show that God must exist and that God was perfect. His arguments went along the following lines:

a. Although he might in deep reflection doubt that he had a body and that there was an independent external world of physical things, nevertheless, despite his best endeavours and the full use of his reason, he could not rid himself of the firm belief that he had a body and that a physical world existed beyond his mind.

b. If there were in reality no physical world, then he would have been grossly deceived all his life.

c. God, who must exist, being perfect in all ways and so perfect in goodness (as had been shown in his earlier proofs) could not be a deceiver.

d. Therefore there must be a physical world of objects including his own body.

Descartes had now constructed, at least to his own satisfaction, his bridge leading from one certainty, his own existence as a thinking thing, to another certainty, the existence of the physical world. European philosophers for another three hundred years, though they might disagree with Descartes on many other issues, broadly agreed with him, at least to this extent, that, first, our initial port of call in the exploration of what exists, of how we should describe reality, is the existence of the mind and, second, that the physical word is, as it were, at a distance, not the object of first-hand knowledge but to be inferred from the first-hand knowledge of our own minds. Consciousness (as is implied in the quotation from Max Planck at the beginning of this chapter) was the intermediary through which we came to know the external world of mountains, trees, houses, bodies and even brains.

I mentioned the simile of the theatre in the introduction. Nowadays we might think in terms of film instead of theatre. What Descartes and philosophers of the generations after him are agreeing on is that the human condition is like sitting in a cinema, that is, each one of us in his or her own private cinema. Our lives, our conscious states, are the films that each of us separately watches; all the events of all our days are the scenes taking place on the screen. This is what we know for sure: we are having conscious experiences, that is, watching the private screening. The compelling task for philosophers who hold this view is to find out if there is a world outside the cinema. In the tradition of British philosophers that came after Descartes there were different answers to this question which can be summarised as follows:

- What takes place on our private screen is similar to the world outside the cinema.
- There is no reason to believe that there is a world outside the cinema.
- It is impossible to resolve the question of whether or not there is a world outside the cinema.

I want next to look at other reasons that do not require any background in the history of philosophy as to why it makes sense to consider consciousness as the given, the primary knowledge and the physical world as secondary.

THE MOTH, THE MOON AND THE STAR

Suppose that George is looking through a window at the night sky. There is no cloud and he sees the moon and beside it many stars against the black background. On the windowpane lands a moth. He can now see moth, moon and stars, all in a single visual experience.

Light travels at 186,000 miles per second. Before we see anything, light must take some time on the journey from the object we see to the eye. I can see through one eye the end of my nose or the rim of my glasses. Because light needs time to pass through space, then even these objects so very close to my eye I see after a brief delay. It may be an infinitesimal fraction of a second but it is a period of time. Time is passing even when light makes this short journey.

The moon is about a quarter of a million miles away. Because light covers that distance in just over a second, when George looks at the moon, he sees it as it was just over a second in the past. As for the stars, the very nearest are several light years away. Millions, billions more stars are decades, centuries and millennia away.

George is sitting at his desk at night looking through the window. In his field of vision is a moth, the moon and a star. In his seeing in one instant he perceives three objects as they were at different points in the past: one at the most a minute fraction of a second ago; one just over a second ago; one, perhaps, a thousand years ago. The conscious experience of seeing is taking place now; it occupies his present moment. But the content of that experience, the objects he appears to be perceiving, are presented to his vision not as they are now but as they were at different times in the past.

In short, the three images appear simultaneously to him but they represent objects as they were at different points in time.

Suppose it were the case that the star he was observing in his field of vision alongside the moon and the moth had ceased to exist five hundred years ago, that about the time Columbus crossed the Atlantic it had exploded, then shrunk to an invisible black hole. It follows that in his present vision one of the objects he is looking at no longer exists. And yet he is seeing it now. Or so it appears.

The inference from this observation is that what we are aware of directly are mental images not things in the outside world. Note that the moth, moon and the now extinct star form the content of a single visual picture observed by George; he is seeing all three in the same instant of time. Is he seeing the star directly? How could he be? But he is seeing something and some explanation needs to be given of what that something, that bright silvery shape, actually is.

These observations support the view that our knowledge is primarily of our own mental states, that they are the given; our knowledge of the world outside us is secondary and dependent on the direct experience of the mental states. We know the world of physical objects by virtue of our mental states.

SENSE-DATA THEORY

Problems of perception such as those raised by the example of the moth, moon and star are grounds for accepting a view of perception called sense-data theory which I would now like to look at more generally. The traditional arguments for it can be grouped under the following headings: variability, illusion and hallucination.

1. VARIABILITY

Our unquestioned common-sense beliefs tell us that grass is green and post boxes are red; it seems obvious that these and other objects have colours just as they have dimensions, a shape and a mass. However, we also remember being surprised at times that the colour of, say, a dress changes when under different light conditions: artificial light in a shop, neon lights in a street and bright sunlight, for example. And of course how bright the light is counts as another factor. The colour of a material as it appears to the viewer even alters to some extent in accordance with its setting. Surround a pink scarf with different collections of reds, blues, oranges or black and the scarf itself seems to take on different shades within the range of pink. And there is also the factor that the quality of colour vision varies from person to person: from those with a sharply discriminating eye to those with severe levels of colour blindness.

On the other hand the shape of the dress and its measurements do not seem to vary in the same way. If we get out a tape measure, we will all agree about the width of the waist and the length of the dress. So as the dress is taken out of the shop into the street and into daylight, we would note its colour changing but its dimensions by contrast do not seem to vary in the same way. So a difference is apparent between the dimensions and the colour of an object.

Suppose George buys a dress for Jane. She does not like it for two reasons: it is the wrong colour and the wrong size. Now George could defend his purchase as regards the colour of the dress. It looked her favourite deep pink in the shop but at home it is more of a red. But he stands no chance of being forgiven for buying a dress of the wrong size. If Jane was a size 10 when he went to the shop, her dimensions will not have altered by the time of his return.

What conclusions can we draw from this difference between the colour and the dimensions of an object? One response is to say that the object, the dress, has in itself certain intrinsic properties, for example, its shape and its measurements. These properties do not vary whoever is looking at it; it makes no difference who is doing the measuring or where the measuring is taking place. The colour of the dress, however, varies from place to place and is to some extent dependent on the quality of vision of the person looking at it and the conditions in which it is being seen. The colour is not intrinsic to or an essential part of the dress in the same way.

An explanation for this difference between unvarying shape and variable colour was suggested by John Locke (1632-1702) who held the view that an object had two types of property: primary and secondary. His position has been much debated, developed and criticised in the succeeding centuries. What follows is a version of his theory not attributable in all details to Locke himself.

The primary properties are those that are in the object itself and do not vary; the secondary are in the mind of the perceiver and vary in accordance with different conditions. So the dimensions of the dress are examples of primary properties, objective facts about the dress; its perceived colour can be classed as a secondary property, a feature both of the mind of the perceiver and of the dress itself.

From these considerations we can begin to see a case for what is called sense-data theory. The implication of variability is that what we are directly aware of is the colour of the dress as it appears to us, our subjective version of colour, as it were. We see the mental picture, an image in the mind rather than the dress itself as it is. An image that is seen in the mind came to be called in twentieth century philosophy a sense datum (sense data in the plural).

Sense-data theory is relevant to the more general concerns of this chapter since it implies that what is known directly or what we are directly acquainted with is the conscious state, in this case the mental image, and that the object itself is known indirectly through the intermediary of the mental image. Again the implication is that the conscious state rather than the physical state is the given. We need to look next at the second argument which introduces the idea of illusions.

2. ILLUSION

In cases of illusion our perception of something is significantly different from the way we think it is in reality. Examples of illusions are numerous and well known. Here are some of them:

a. the way a straight stick looks as if it is bent when placed in glass bowl of water
b. the way that the moon appears much larger when it is near to the horizon than it does when it is higher in the sky
c. simple perspective: the fact that objects like buildings or people look smaller in the distance than they do when closer to us
d. the way railway lines appear to converge as we look further into the distance

In all these cases what we actually perceive is not what our reason tells us is reality in a world outside the mind. The implication is that we do not see the world as it is, that there is a distinction between its appearance and its reality. Appearance is the direct object of our sense perception; it is the world seen from the first-person viewpoint. Reality, the way the world is 'out there' (or from the third-person viewpoint), we come to know indirectly.

Sense-data theory helps us make sense of this appearance/ reality distinction. As we saw in the case of variability, it holds that we do not perceive objects in our surroundings directly but indirectly via mental images of them. Imagine that George is a passenger in a car spending a whole journey staring only at the mirror and never once looking outside the car at the passing scene. He does not see trees, houses, fields and traffic directly but what he actually sees is a series of reflections of them in the mirror. According to sense-data theory our situation is comparable to that of George. The sense data are like the reflections in the mirror; in both cases there is a separate reality which is similar to what is perceived.

These images or sense data in this analysis of illusions are like what is outside us but not identical with it. For example, in the classic case of the stick that appears to bend in water, what we perceive is the mental picture in which the stick is bent and that mental picture resembles the reality of the situation; there is a stick and water in the world beyond the mind but with the significant difference that out there it is straight. This view that inwardly perceived sense data resemble the outer reality of physical objects came to be known as representative realism.

In the context of the cinema analogy mentioned in reference to Descartes, representative realism holds that the film we are watching on our private screening is a personal, subjective version of the story taking place outside the cinema in a real world of physical objects.

3. HALLUCINATION

Hallucinations probably do not feature much in the experience of most of us. We tend to think of them, perhaps, as linked to the culture of 1960s' experiments with LSD and similar drugs. Or we remember from our school days Macbeth crying,

'Is this a dagger that I see before me, the handle toward my hand?', a fevered mind of a guilt-ridden man seeing an object which he could not touch because it did not exist. But we all know what it is like to have dreams. And in our dreams we see people, places, shapes and colours, objects at rest or in motion; we hear voices, doorbells, the wind in the leaves and so on.

In these cases, drug induced hallucinations and everynight dreams, we are certainly having conscious experiences. We are seeing, we are hearing, touching, perhaps having tastes and smells and emotional states too. At the time of the experiences their reality is not in question. But the significant point is that they correspond to nothing that is happening in the world outside the mind.

The situation as regards variability and illusion is very different. Here what is perceived does correspond to an external reality. We see subjectively the colour of a dress that really exists outside the mind; we see subjectively a bent stick which is our inner version of a straight stick which really exists outside us.

But hallucinations and dreams do not resemble anything going on at that time beyond the experience. If we return briefly to the cinema metaphor, in these cases each one of us is in a private cinema and what is taking place on the screen is not a distorted copy or in any way related to a series of events taking place outside the cinema. It is just a film running. On its own. Out of nowhere.

What is it we are perceiving in hallucinations and dreams, experiences which, at the time they are taking place, are as real to us as veridical experiences, that is, experiences that represent the world in a basically truthful way? Again sense-data theory offers an answer. What we are perceiving are images in the mind, the content of our conscious experiences.

All these considerations as regards variability, illusions and hallucinations reinforce the view that what we really know directly, at first hand, without intermediary of any kind is consciousness, our ever changing and fleeting conscious experiences. Consciousness, not the world of physical objects, is surely our first base, the given of our enquiry?

THE ELECTRODE EXPERIMENT

Go back to the analysis in Chapter 1 of the process involved in seeing a tree when we traced the stages from light being reflected on to the eye to the receipt of information in the processing system of the visual cortex. George is again the subject. His brain is in a particular state at the point in time at which he sees the tree: particular neurons are firing in there; we do not know precisely which ones but it is a reasonable inference that there has been a neural change of some kind in response to this visual stimulus. The brain is now in the precise physical state which corresponds to George's seeing-the-tree experience.

Imagine that the attainment of that particular configuration of firing neurons is compared to the flipping of a switch. The switch is in off-position until the new data has entered and been processed in the visual cortex which has the effect of pressing it into the on-position. When the switch is off, George does not see the tree; when the switch is on (the right neurons are firing at the right rate), George does see the tree.

Now we add a new element. George is lying on a couch in a university psychology department. Surrounding him is a group of scientists attaching electrodes to his head. They have very precisely fine-tuned the electrical input so that the effect will be to flip the switch inside George's head from off to on. So by artificial means they have put George's brain into exactly the same state it was in when he saw the tree. Will he see a tree now even though there is no tree in his vicinity to be seen?

What will happen from George's point of view? The configuration of the neurons in George's brain controlled by the electrodes is a perfect copy of the configuration of neurons in his brain at the time when he saw the tree. Does George now see the tree? Intuitively, it seems that he must. But on this occasion there is no tree present before him to be seen. He is in effect experiencing a hallucination.

At both times, during the veridical experience (when the tree is actually being seen) and the hallucinatory experience (when there is no tree), George is having qualitatively the same experience. To him there is no detectable difference between the two phenomena. Does this thought experiment not imply very strongly that we perceive directly mental images or sense data rather than physical objects?

But in fact we do not have to resort to thought experiments to make this point. I mentioned the Canadian neuroscientist, Wilder Penfield (1891-1976) in Chapter 2. In the course of his efforts to treat patients for epilepsy he exposed those parts of their brains where he believed the seizures to be focussed. The patients, given only a local anaesthetic in the scalp, remained conscious throughout the treatment. When Penfield applied an electrode to the surface of the exposed brain, the results went far beyond his expectations. The patients became aware of what they described as flashbacks to earlier waking experiences as if the electrode had in some way stimulated a memory brought to the forefront of conscious awareness. For example, a mother reported being in her kitchen hearing the voice of her child playing outside and the sound of cars. Other patients reported being at a sports event or at a concert. Not all the experiences were of memory: one patient felt a tingling in her thumb or in her tongue when different parts of her brain were stimulated. Penfield wrote about his work in *The Mystery of the Mind: A Critical Study of Consciousness and the Human Brain* (1975) as follows:

'The stimulating current was increased from two to three volts. The succeeding responses from the temporal lobe were "psychical" instead of sensory or motor. They were activations of the stream of consciousness from the past as follows. (The numbers refer to the parts of the brain labelled and stimulated):

11 – "I heard something, I do not know what it was."

11 – (repeated without warning) "Yes, Sir, I think I heard a mother calling her little boy somewhere. It seemed to be something that happened years ago." When asked to explain, she said, "It was somebody in the neighborhood where I live." Then she added that she herself "was somewhere close enough to hear."

12 – "Yes. I heard voices down along the river somewhere – a man's voice and a woman's voice calling ... I think I saw the river."

15 – "Just a tiny flash of a feeling of familiarity and a feeling that I knew everything that was going to happen in the near future."

17c – (A needle insulated except at the tip was inserted to
the superior surface of the temporal lobe, deep in the fissure
of Sylvius and the current was switched on.) "Oh! I had the
same very, very familiar memory, in an office somewhere. I
could see the desks. I was there and someone was calling
to me, a man leaning on a desk with a pencil in his hand."

I warned her I was going to stimulate,
but I did not do so. "Nothing."

18a – (stimulation without warning) "I had a little
memory – scene in a play – they were talking and I
could see it – I was just seeing it in my memory." '

Penfield's experiments took place a long time ago. Is there
more up-to-date evidence to back them up? A paper in an
edition of the journal *Neurology* published in 2000 reinforces
Penfield's revelations. When the occipital cortex and adjacent
cortices were stimulated (again in epilepsy patients), the
patients reported having visual experiences of shape, colour
and motion.

What both Penfield's and the more recent research confirm
is that people can have sense experiences when the brain is
put into a particular state. First, those experiences do not have
to originate in the sensory organs as the result of input from
the environment. Second, those experiences are really taking
place; the patients are directly aware of them. Nothing was
causing the woman's arm and tongue to tingle when she had
those feelings; no objects with shape, colour and motion were
reflecting light on to the eyes of the patients who had visual
experiences of shape, colour and motion. And yet they were

undoubtedly feeling or seeing something. Is there any other theory that even comes near to offering an explanation? And if it is sense data that are the direct objects of our perception (rather than physical objects outside the mind), then the view that consciousness is what we know directly, first and foremost, is confirmed.

THE ELECTRO-MAGNETIC SPECTRUM

Light, on which all our visual experiences depend, can be thought of as a wave moving at 186,000 miles per second. But the light to which our eyes are sensitive is a particular segment of a wide range of waves called the electro-magnetic spectrum. The longest of these waves, several kilometres across, radio waves, are used in radio, television and mobile phone communication. Next in width come microwaves which agitate liquids and so can be used to create heat in cooking. After infra-red, a wavelength used in some types of photography, comes the range of waves that matter for human vision, the visible spectrum. Wavelengths shorter than the visible range are ultraviolet rays, x-rays (which, since they pass through flesh but not bone, are a very useful aid in medical treatment) and the very short gamma rays.

The way the world appears depends on the conditions under which it is seen. For whatever reason we humans have eyes which respond to this small section of the spectrum. As a consequence we see bananas as yellow, cherries as red, grass as green and so on. But if we had different types of eyes, ones that responded to a different segment of the spectrum then the way the world appeared to us would be different. The eyes of honey bees are sensitive to ultra violet light; presumably, their conscious experience of the colours of flowers is different at least to the extent of their having this extra facility. And with the aid of specialised cameras (used in night time photography by naturalists, the police and spies) we can see how the world appears in infra-red light.

We can speculate about extra-terrestrial visitors whose eyes might be sensitive to other wavelengths of radiation, say, microwaves or x-rays. The environment as it appears to us might appear to be very different to them. Imagine having your eyes permanently adapted to be sensitive to x-rays! What each observer, whether honey bee, human or Martian actually sees is shaped by the nature of their seeing apparatus. In each case the observer is having a visual conscious experience. The visual experience of colour or of whatever sort is the direct object of their perception.

The fact that each observer with different visual equipment has a different visual experience is quite consistent with the idea that there exists independently of them all a physical world that can be seen in different ways. But the example of the electromagnetic spectrum reinforces the point made earlier that we have direct access to the appearance in the conscious experience and that the physical object observed is known indirectly.

THE BISCUIT TIN

I have in front of me a biscuit tin, a biscuit tin that is a cylinder shape. We all know what a cylinder is; we can describe it, think about it, even rotate it or turn it upside down in the imagination. A cylinder is a three dimensional object with a circular base and top, a sort of collection of joined up circles on top of one another But when I stop to look at the biscuit tin, really look at it, that is, what do I actually see? It is part of the training of artists to learn how to look. It is important for them to start to see things — the bowl of fruit, the model — without preconceptions, to observe as much as is possible what is actually before their eyes. The untrained eye misses so much. How many of us notice the wallpaper, the furniture, our surroundings in general? We forget how to look.

If I stop to look at the biscuit tin — really look at it, I mean — a cylinder is not the shape that I actually see directly before me. From above I see a circle and that circle blends into an oval as I move away; from the side I see a rectangle and so on. But never a cylinder.

As a child how did I find out what a cylinder was? I was not born with a ready-made concept of a cylinder in my mind. As I came in and out of a room, perhaps I looked at a biscuit tin like this one many times, seeing it from many different angles, from close to, from the far side of the room. Presumably, I stored, in my mind, quite unconsciously, a collection of these visual snapshots and on the basis of these there arose in my mind something different from them, the concept of a cylinder. After a while I could imagine what the biscuit tin would look like if it fell upside down on the floor or was hanging from the ceiling. A cylinder is not really something we see directly but an idea we come to understand.

The metaphor of a snapshot was useful a moment ago. When all day long we are looking at things in our surroundings the door, the window, cars, shops and so on, it is as if we are snapping thousands and thousands of photographs. Take the house we leave in the morning and return to in the evening. We see it from outside the front door, from the street, from different parts of the garden; we might even see it from a helicopter! Our idea of the house is not any single one of these separate photographs but a concept that has been formed as some sort of distillation or summary of these photographs. From my concept of the house, I can visualise what it looks like from different angles and from different distances. I can even imagine how it would seem from points of view I have not actually occupied. A house, like the biscuit tin, is a concept that has been built up from many pictures taken from different perspectives.

And what is true of how we learn about the biscuit tin and the house is true, surely, of how we learn about all physical objects. Our ideas of them are constructed out of a range of, mainly, visual information collected over time. This way of explaining how we come to have ideas of objects in the world around us is called phenomenalism. (The word comes from the sense of 'phenomenon' meaning appearance.) Phenomenalism is concerned with how we assemble an idea of an object on the basis of the way it has appeared to us in a series of separate pictures. To the phenomenalist what we mean by the term 'biscuit tin' is all the different snapshots of the biscuit tin plus all the possible ones. 'Objects are the permanent possibilities of sensation,' wrote JS Mill (1809-1873).

Phenomenalism begins with consciousness. It tries to stay within our experience, what we actually perceive, and to make sense of what we consider to be an independent world of objects without departing from that direct experience. In recent years it has come under a great deal of criticism which is not my immediate concern here. There is certainly plenty to discuss about phenomenalism. But all I want to introduce here is the way that phenomenalism offers another approach to addressing reality from the consciousness-first viewpoint.

FLAMES AND COAL

Look for a few minutes at a fire burning, at the flames and coal. The flames flicker, rise, fall, suddenly appear, quickly disappear, vary in colour. The coal, however, looks like a model of consistency in comparison, changing slowly, almost imperceptibly in the moments you devote to it, as if it occupied a different domain of time from that of the flames. An elephant surrounded by brightly coloured dragonflies.

Like flames conscious experiences seem unstable, variable, fleeting, insecure whereas physical things, whether mountains or brains seem, like the coal, solid, comparatively permanent, hard, concrete and most definitely real.

It is our habit to think of matter and consciousness in such terms: the flimsy, wispy, delicate tumbledown quality of consciousness in contrast with the granite, substantial permanence of lumps of matter. So when we meet unfamiliar theories, such as phenomenalism, theories which position consciousness first in knowledge, which regard consciousness not matter as the direct object of knowledge, then we naturally tend to be suspicious. And we rightly ask about consciousness where does it come from, how can it be accounted for, what keeps it coherent. For example, what holds together the smell, the colour, the shape, the taste of an orange, all those conscious experiences in the absence of an orange existing independently of the mind. Consciousness is surely too insubstantial to be floating free and to exist on its own; it must depend on something more enduring than itself, arise out of something more fixed and rooted than it is in itself. In short, we can hardly help assuming that consciousness emerges from or grows out of or in some way needs for its very existence the physical body and the brain. We cannot make any sense of the flames without the coal.

But is matter really in a more privileged position than consciousness? What gives matter the property of being fixed and permanent? How does it retain its form as mountain, rock, body or brain? We require that a set of conscious experiences should have a basis outside itself, some external adhesive to hold it together but we do not ordinarily require of matter that it too should have a basis outside itself to hold it together.

Back to consciousness and matter. What I am addressing here is our prejudice in favour of matter. We expect of consciousness that there is beyond it that which accounts for it. We do not think that is can be self-sufficient, the *causa sui* (the cause of itself). We fail to ask the same question of matter presumably because we don't think that it requires an explanation. Matter just is. But is that a reasonable assumption? Surely we can ask the same question of matter we ask of consciousness?

Throughout this chapter I have been attempting to show that what I called in the Introduction the Physical-First approach to understanding consciousness is mistaken. It takes as the given the physical which under closer analysis is not able to fulfil that role. Time after time we have seen that the basis of our understanding of reality and of our understanding of what we ourselves actually are must begin with the indisputable fact of consciousness. As the great scientist, Max Planck, put it, 'We cannot get behind consciousness'.

CHAPTER 6

BACK TO MATTER

INTRODUCTION

The trend in philosophical literature during recent decades is, as we have seen, to take the physical as the given and to attempt to accommodate consciousness within its parameters. The physical is very widely regarded as the unquestioned basis of discussion. I do not remember reading in any of the texts on the philosophy of mind and the mind-body problem a discussion of the nature of matter itself, any serious doubts about the security of matter as the reliable foundation. As you go through these texts, looking at chapter headings and at the index, it would never occur to you that the nature of matter presented any philosophical problems at all. It is always consciousness that is the awkward difficulty. I remember the comic chestnut which made fun of the parochialism of the English, 'Fog in the channel. Continent cut off', the point being, of course, that a certain strain in the English mind was totally convinced that England was so obviously the centrepiece of the world that Europe could be considered a mere offshore island. There is a similar mindset amongst some philosophers. To them materiality is, metaphorically and literally, the rock-solid ground on which to build their intellectual structures. Consciousness, by contrast, is the rather vague and difficult-to-pin down other, the nuisance that needs to be brought to order, the recalcitrant black sheep they must rehabilitate into the happy ontological family. To me it makes more sense to think of consciousness as Europe which encompasses England. It is the materialist philosophers, I suggest, who are the philosophical chauvinists.

Strangely, it is science, the body of knowledge that might appear to be so securely rooted in materiality, rather than philosophy itself, that raises doubts, very serious doubts about any comfortable notions we might have concerning the nature of matter. It does not take much enquiry (and you do not need to be a professional scientist to do it) to have good reason to wonder whether we really do know enough about matter to give it the lofty status of the given. Probably, the first feature of matter that fades under closer inspection is the idea of its solidity. And soon, as the enquiry progresses, the nature of matter becomes more and more mysterious.

THE EMPTINESS OF MATTER

The idea that all physical objects are composed of infinitesimally small bits of matter can be traced back at least to Democritus (to whom I referred in Chapter 3) in the Greece of the fifth century BC. It was thought that matter on the large scale was divisible but that if you continued to cut it into smaller and smaller pieces, you would ultimately find that there were units that could not be split into anything smaller. These were the atoms. Atomic theory has then a very long history.

The understanding of atoms in terms of more practical science came much later. Dalton reached the conclusion in 1808 that the existence of atoms was the best explanation of the fact that elements always combined with one another in simple proportions. But the assumption that the atom was a solid lump of material began to fade at the end of the nineteenth century. In 1897 J J Thompson, in discovering electrons, showed that atoms had constituent parts. Eight years later Rutherford's experiments with gold foil implied that the atom resembled a miniature solar system with electrons (like planets) revolving around and at a great distance from a nucleus (the sun). Subsequent theory cast in doubt this analogy but let us leave that development and stop at this point to dwell on what an atom is like.

Most of the mass of an atom consists of its nucleus which is made up of protons and neutrons. But what is surprising about the atom is how small this nucleus turns out to be in comparison with the size of the whole atom. The diameter of the atom is 200,000 times the width of the nucleus.

Now in the first place it takes some effort of imagination to grasp just how small an atom itself is. A human hair is about one million atoms wide; a speck of dust might contain three trillion atoms. But not just hair and dust, of course, every physical object in the universe is made of these atoms so minute it is hardly possible to imagine them: stars, mountains, trees, houses and, of course, our bodies, including every bit of our brains. And next we have to recognise that every one of these countless atoms contains a minute centre surrounded by an immense void. Each one is almost totally empty.

There are two implication of the nature of the atom I would like to pursue. First, it is obvious that the world around us does not look and feel as if it were nearly all empty space. Indeed, some of it, like a concrete floor or a brick wall, feels very distinctly solid. The difference between the way the world appears to our senses and the way the world is revealed in the close inspection of scientific enquiry recalls the discussion of sense data theory in Chapter 5.

When I look at a wall, I see no holes in it; when I touch the wall, it feels solid. These observations are easily accommodated within sense-data theory as follows: I am having conscious experiences of seeing (visual sense data) and touching (tactile sense data) which I know directly; the existence of the wall as a physical object existing beyond my mind is inferred from those conscious states. Our direct awareness of the way the world appears to the senses in our conscious experiences is different from the way the world is revealed to be on the basis of scientific analysis. The view that conscious states are primary and that physical objects are secondary is reinforced by the analysis of matter which proves to be a great void inhabited by the merest specks of particles.

Second, matter, taken to be the given of contemporary discussion in philosophy of mind debates, now looks an even less likely candidate to be one and the same thing as consciousness or to be the cause of consciousness. We now know that every one of our hundred billion neurons in the brain is a virtual void. Even before we discovered this fact, we had no way of answering the question how could neurons be conscious states or be the cause of conscious states. But now a harder question must be put. How can a brain of one hundred billion cells, each one made of millions of almost empty atoms be identical with, or be the cause of, our taste and sound experiences, our thoughts and feelings? How do we bridge the gap between tiny dots in great oceans of empty space and the vivid richness of consciousness?

QUANTUM THEORY

It is difficult enough to get a grip both on the idea that the universe is an almost total vacuum and also on the idea that the virtually empty atoms which make up our brains can somehow generate out of themselves the stuff of conscious experience. However, even this later model of the physical universe as a solar system in miniature in which tiny pieces of matter called electrons, real, solid, objective things, like minute ball bearings or marbles spinning in some elaborate sub-atomic dance round a fixed centre, the nucleus, is itself long past its sell-by-date. And it is important to reaffirm here that the demolition of the traditional and comfortable picture of a universe as a place that is a dependably real, understandable and sure basis on which to build an enquiry into an, apparently, more flimsy and elusive consciousness has been accomplished by scientists themselves. It has not been an intrusion of innumerate and scientifically illiterate philosophers that has undermined the received wisdom of science but the work of the most sophisticated and revered practitioners of science itself.

There is a rich historical irony in the juxtaposition of philosophical movements and scientific developments. The first half of the twentieth century saw the rise of logical positivism in philosophy simultaneous with the emergence of the new science of quantum physics. Philosophy was making a break with its past: the construction of teetering towers of extravagant metaphysical systems that had been the concern of philosophers from Plato to Hegel was rejected in favour of a much more limited role for philosophy. Logical positivism set out its verification principle: only propositions that were empirically verifiable were to be considered meaningful. It followed that propositions about ethics (euthanasia is good or bad, for instance), aesthetics (this painting is more beautiful than that painting, for instance), religion (God is love, for instance) and metaphysics (the world is mind-dependent, for instance), since there was no empirical evidence against which they could be checked, were by this criterion deemed meaningless. Science par excellence was devoted to and demonstrably successful in the empirical investigation of what purported to be reality, for the hypotheses of science, since they could be tested, were verifiable. Within the confines of a verification principle science so effectively dominated that there was little work remaining for philosophy to do. Philosophy was demoted. It had enjoyed a long reign as queen of intellectual disciplines — remember that science or natural philosophy as it used to be called had initially been a branch of philosophy before it proclaimed its independence. Philosophy was now relegated to the lowly status of handmaiden to science, its comparatively menial task to clarify concepts, clean up untidy areas of language and collect what other crumbs fell from the scientific benches.

Simultaneously, physics, still reeling from the mind-blowing revelations of relativity, was confronted with even stranger theories that seriously threatened the traditional understanding of the physical universe. In one of the greatest misjudgements of the course of the future Lord Kelvin had written in 1894 'There is nothing new to be discovered in physics now. All that remains is more and more precise measurement.' It was an axiom of physics supported by common sense that the universe, comparable to a gigantic clockwork mechanism operating deterministically on cause-and-effect principles, existed independently of any observations. In short, there was a universe out there, whether I was aware of it or not, and it consisted of real, solid things which obeyed to the last atom the laws of nature. These laws had been discovered and meticulously described by Newton and his successors. Physics, apparently, had now no major task to carry out. This completely deterministic universe was also, in theory, a completely predictable one, a conclusion famously drawn by the French thinker, Laplace:

'We ought to regard the present state of the universe as the effect of its antecedent state and as the cause of the state that is to follow. An intelligence knowing all the forces acting in nature at a given instant, as well as the momentary positions of all things in the universe, would be able to comprehend in one single formula the motions of the largest bodies as well as the lightest atoms in the world, provided that its intellect were sufficiently powerful to subject all data to analysis; to it nothing would be uncertain, the future as well as the past would be present to its eyes. The perfection that the human mind has been able to give to astronomy affords but a feeble outline of such an intelligence.' (1820)

What Kelvin had no reason to predict were the two revolutions that took place in physics in the early years of the twentieth century: relativity and quantum theory. It is quantum theory in particular that relates to the nature of the physical, to the question of what we mean by matter and it is to this science that I now turn. I must recall at this point that this book is not a scientific enquiry at all and only touches on science in what some may consider a very rudimentary way for the following reason. As I mentioned earlier, time after time in books, articles and discussions about the mind, it is the mind that is presented as a difficult anomaly. The physical world, by contrast, is not considered to be a problem in philosophy of mind studies: it is the ground where you begin and what you take for granted. It is the place of consciousness in the given physical universe that is always regarded as the besetting difficulty. Granted that there are real things from sub-atomic particles to galaxies, what account can we give for feelings and thoughts and sense experiences? Where do they come from? These are the questions you meet time after time.

My position in this chapter takes issue with this starting assumption. I am introducing some scientific material because the job of science is to study the nature of matter, and, from what scientists themselves have discovered, the physical universe is proving to be anything but the sure, certain, understandable basis that can be quietly taken for granted as a framework into which the mysteries of consciousness have to be assimilated. Quantum physics is notoriously difficult, however, and I make no claim whatsoever to have understood it. Even scientists themselves are willing to admit to being bewildered by its complexities and paradoxes (though I am sure their bewilderment is very much better informed and at a much higher level than mine). Below I list some of the conclusions reached by quantum physicists about the nature of matter at the level of the particles that make up the atom.

- that the location of a particle is determined by the event of observation
- that therefore before the observation takes place the particle is potentially in more than one place
- that, in short: 'observations not only disturb what is to be measured, they produce it.' Pascual Jordan (physicist, 1909-1980)

- that the more accurate is the measure of the location of an object the more uncertain is the measure of its velocity (and vice versa).

- that scientific realism, implying in this context the idea of sub-atomic particles as tiny bits of solid stuff existing independently of our knowledge of them, needs to be abandoned: 'atoms or elementary particles themselves are not real; they form a world of potentialities or possibilities rather than one of things or facts.' Werner Heisenberg, physicist (1901-1976)

I hope that the irony I mentioned is now evident. How strange it seems now as we look back into the early years of the twentieth century that so much faith was being put by academic philosophers into the scientific understanding of reality at the very time that the underpinnings of its most fundamental area, physics, were being demolished in a way that opened up fundamentally challenging philosophical problems.

There are several points to be drawn out of these findings. It is certainly true, first, that some scientists dispute the conclusions as regards scientific realism and, second, that many scientists use quantum physics as a very well established discipline which allows great progress to be made in a purely scientific understanding as well as in a vast and important area of technology without their feeling any need to pursue its more philosophical implications.

But the fact remains that the understanding of the physical universe has been revolutionised in the twentieth century. Before quantum physics the question was how do we accommodate consciousness into the well understood domain of physicality: after quantum physics we ask the question how can it be that a conscious event, an act of observation can determine the way the physical world behaves. It seems that the relationship between matter and consciousness has to be understood on a new level of complexity. The nature of matter is just as much the problem now.

Surely what we must now jettison is the hackneyed problem found in traditional mind philosophy. It cannot be seriously be contended almost a century after the major discoveries of quantum physics that the physical universe is the safe, sure, comfortable beginning for a venture into the tricky area of consciousness. What could be more problematic than our understanding of the physical world post-quantum physics? It is a mystery just as consciousness is a mystery.

RESTORATION OF MATTER
THE GLOBE

Imagine that in a school geography lesson a globe is placed on a table around which sit twenty students. Each student looking at the globe sees a different segment of it. One sees the Atlantic with parts of Europe, Africa and North and South America; someone else sees the Pacific with parts of China, Japan and Australia. Each of the twenty students, depending on where he or she is sitting, sees a particular segment of the globe. Next the teacher turns the globe ten times in one direction, Time_1 to Time_{10}. As a consequence what each student sees changes ten times. This all seems very obvious. There is a physical object, the globe, which stage by stage is being rotated and, as a consequence, it is easy to explain which part of the globe is in their view.

Now look at the situation again on the assumption that there are only conscious states, that there is no globe existing independently of the minds of the students, in other words in phenomenalist terms. In the mind of each student is a set of seeing-the-globe sense data (seeing-the-Atlantic, seeing-the-Pacific sense data, for example). In the conscious experience of each student is a particular pattern of colours, shapes and words showing land and water etc. What happens when the teacher moves the globe an inch or so in one direction in the stages from T_1 to T_{10}? It seems now that in each visual experience the particular pattern of colours and shapes has changed: there is, perhaps, a little more blue (for sea) in one, a little more green (for land) in another.

But, significantly, even though there is in this thought experiment no physical globe existing independently of the minds, nevertheless those sets of sense data, those particular patterns of colour and shape in the twenty minds at each of the ten stages of movement are perfectly consistent with the existence of a physical globe existing out there in a real physical world. And if some of the students in this phenomenalist world were to posit the existence of such an object existing outside their minds, they would be able to calculate exactly what details and boundaries of land and ocean form the content of the sense data in their own and in the other minds at each stage of the turning. The assumption that there was indeed a globe in the room would be the most effective way of calculating what each student would see at each point in time from T_1 to T_{10}.

Furthermore, the example can easily be altered so as to require even more complex calculations which would all work with just the same accuracy. Imagine instead of twenty observers round a globe, a thousand (or, for that matter, a million) satellites around the earth, all constantly in motion and all continually photographing the earth. The particular portion of the earth's surface visible on each photograph is calculable on the basis of measurements of speed, distance and angle.

My point is this. It actually makes much more sense of the situation to assume that over and above all the direct visual experiences there is in the middle of a group of people a piece of materiality called a globe or the earth. Once I employ the model that there is a globe or the earth 'out there', I can work out what is being perceived and foresee what will be perceived from all the different viewpoints. Such calculations and predictions regularly prove to be reliable. If we take physical objects to have independent existence, we now have some sort of an explanation for the variety of sense data.

If I walk up the high street of a town, I pass a butcher's, a chemist's, a side street, a church and a pub. When I walk down the high street in the opposite direction, I pass the same buildings in reverse order. Common sense if we take for granted a fixed and independent physical world. From the point of view of phenomenalism, however, according to which I have seeing-a-butcher's-shop visual experience followed by seeing-a-chemist's-shop and so on experiences, it is very difficult to make sense of what is happening. For some reason I would be having one set of visual experiences on the journey out and the same experiences in reverse order on the journey back. Why, if there is no street there? The best explanation of my experiences is surely that there is external to me an actual physical object, the high street.

SYNCHRONISATION

George and Jane are having a conversation. Jane both hears George's voice and sees his lips moving. Nothing very remarkable with that. However, hearing and seeing, since they are two discrete types of sense perception, could each occur in the absence of the other. Hearing a voice is a sense experience we can easily separate from seeing lips move. If we now consider the situation in phenomenalist terms, Jane is experiencing two distinct sets of sense data, sound and sight and there is no George's body existing independently. The synchronization of the sense data of sound and sight, however, has sustained precision; there is perfect correlation.

We are familiar with and easily able to identify an error in film projection where the sound of the voices and the lip movements are even slightly 'out of sync'. But in Jane's dual perceptions, seeing and hearing, there is never a moment when lip movements (particularly where most noticeable at the beginning and end of sections of speech) are not perfectly aligned with sound.

Now if there is no physical object (George) existing outside the mind of Jane, this is a very remarkable occurrence. How can it be that sight and sound experiences are so perfectly correlated without the assumption of a common cause, i.e., George's body? We might speculate how in a purely phenomenalist world, a world of consciousness and no material things, such immaculate correspondence might come about. What sort of planning and sophisticated organisation could effect it? But once we adopt the model of the independent existence of a physical world we find that the situation fits neatly into place. If we assume a real George outside Jane's mind, whose lips are moving as they emit sound, then the correlation now makes perfectly good sense.

The point of the examples is not to give a direct proof of a physical world but to show that if we presuppose its existence we can explain connections between our conscious states and predict future conscious states. The belief that there is an independent world of physical objects is a model whereby we can begin to give some sort of an explanation not of the making of consciousness but of the way that conscious states are constantly changing.

NEURAL CORRELATES

Once we accept that there is an independent physical world of mountains, houses and, most important, human bodies with brains, we can try to get some sort of a grip on the relationship between the physical and consciousness. I have tried to show in earlier chapters that the physical is not identical with nor the cause of consciousness. But once it is accepted that the physical exists alongside or in addition to consciousness, then it seems clear that there is a close correlation between them.

What can we say about this correlation? Well, in the first place there is an obviousness to it in the following sense. We smell a flower, that is, have the conscious experience of the fragrance, after we have come close to the flower and something emitted by the flower has been taken into the body. We taste the Marmite after the piece of toast has entered the mouth. It seems more than likely that when we have these sense experiences, they occur after the body has taken in some input from the world around us. If we add a little background about the way light is reflected from objects like trees and the way musical instruments cause vibrations in the air, we find this idea confirmed. It seems that for consciousness of sense experiences the body has first to be affected by some material change via the sensory organs. In a similar way we find that some emotional states (for example, fear) are correlated with the release of hormonal fluids (for example, adrenalin) in the body. But can we go further than this?

In the light of twentieth century advances in human biology we can track the input from the sensory organs to the brain. In Chapter 1 I followed through the process of seeing a tree, looking at the stages that are involved from the outside of the eye to the visual cortex. The correlation looks as though it must be between consciousness and the brain. But is it possible to be more precise? Can it be said which parts of the brain are and which parts are not correlations of consciousness? We are looking for the NCC, the neural correlates of consciousness.

There have been many attempts to identify the NCC, to pick out which parts of the brain, which collections of neurons are the counterparts of consciousness. One approach is to see if the state of the brain is different when a person is in a conscious state from when a person is in an unconscious state, for example, asleep, in a coma or in a persistent vegetative state. Other research has examined anaesthetics, from chloroform and nitrous oxide to modern chemicals used in surgery. Anaesthetics block consciousness and seem to offer an opportunity to observe the brain in a conscious and an unconscious state. Neither approach, however, has revealed a clear-cut distinction that would allow researchers to pinpoint the NCC. It certainly does not seem to be the case that there is a particular area of the brain that is exclusively responsible for consciousness.

The concept of a consciousness threshold seems to hold out some hope in the search for a physical basis. The body can be affected by a stimulus which is not apparent to consciousness. Here are two examples:

a. A word is flashed before a subject on a screen for a very small fraction of a second, enough time for the eye to take in the data and pass it on to the brain but an insufficient time for the subject to be aware of seeing the word.
b. The skin of a subject is touched very lightly, perhaps on the small of the back which is an insensitive area of the body. The body registers the contact but the subject does not feel it.

In both cases the input is below the threshold of consciousness. Now suppose that in each case the level of input is increased:

a. The word is exposed for an increasingly long duration.
b. The contact with the skin is increasingly strong.

Now the subject is a) aware of seeing the word and b) aware of feeling the pressure on the skin.

If the subject's brain is being monitored by a scan throughout this process, observers should be able to note any difference in the state of the brain at two times, below the threshold and above the threshold of consciousness. This seems a promising way to identify the elusive NCC, the precise form of the physical basis that matches conscious states.

Unfortunately, again, there is not as yet conclusive evidence of any clear-cut dividing line between the 'unconscious brain' and the 'conscious brain'. Activity in the neurons increases the greater the input into the body but a sharp difference between the two brain states in addition to the raised level of activity has not emerged.

Instead of trying to find the correlates of consciousness in general, other work has been undertaken to identify the correlates of a particular type of conscious state. In the case of vision it would seem clear that the visual cortex is involved but there is so much activity in that part of the brain, so much processing of information most of which we are not in the slightest way conscious, again it has proved virtually impossible to say which areas of the activity are directly related to the conscious state of seeing.

Pain, the subject of part of Chapter 1, is perhaps the conscious state which has most successfully been correlated with a physical state. It seems that when we are in pain, c-fibres which are specialised thin, unmyelinated neurons are particularly active. Indeed, there is the additional evidence that there seems to be close correspondence between the degree of pain felt and the amount of c-fibre activity. In conclusion, although the assumption of regular correspondence between conscious states and brain events seems sound enough, the NCCs have proved very elusive.

CONCLUSION

This book is an enquiry into the problematic relationship between mind (in particular, consciousness) and the body (in particular, the brain), a problem that is very ancient in origin but is being addressed today at the cutting edge of philosophy, psychology and neuroscience. As noted earlier, the prevailing view of our age is physicalist; it is very widely held that physical things are the fundamental basis of reality and against this background consciousness is considered to be an anomaly. Attempts to explain consciousness within this predominantly physicalist framework are many and varied. Chapters 3 and 4 examined some of these attempts and showed them to be, in my view, wholly inadequate: we did not find an explanation for conscious experiences in terms of brain states. In Chapter 5 I tried to show that this whole project was misconceived and that the fundamental nature of reality, in the sense of what we most certainly know, is consciousness itself and that, contrary to received thinking, it was the physical world about which we come to know indirectly. In short, I argued that consciousness is the given and that the physical is inferred from it.

This chapter has had two objectives. First, the analysis of matter in two stages has further undermined any claims it might have to be a secure foundation in philosophy of mind studies. But, second, in a movement in the opposite direction, is the implication that we do need the notion of a physical world separate from consciousness in order to make sense of the fact that our conscious experiences are in a constant state of change. I hope to have shown that the notion of an independent physical world constitutes a model that, though not proven, is nevertheless the best working hypothesis available to us.

What point have we reached? Of the fact that there is consciousness there can be no doubt: that there is a separate domain of bodies and brains is a very plausible assumption. But how, then, are we to explain the relationship between the two?

I have rejected the claim that consciousness is identical with the brain as quite unfounded. The weaker claim that the brain is the cause of consciousness is more persuasive and deserves more serious attention. As explained earlier, it needs to be broken down into two distinct parts:

a. cause in the sense of the brain out of itself generating or manufacturing consciousness
b. cause in the sense of regular correlation leaving open whether that correlation is causal or occasional.

The first alternative, like the notion of mind-brain identity is ungrounded. There is not the slightest reason to believe that ganglions of cells fizzing with electrical charge and swirling with chemical exchanges should create out of their very dubious physical substance the spectrum of conscious experiences: fragrance to nausea, vivid colours and shade, dread and exultation, the basest of desires and most spiritual of aspirations.

The second alternative, however, has the backing of considerable evidence of correlation. It may not at the present time be possible to identify, except in a few instances, particular conscious states with particular brain states but the case for a regular correspondence between the two is very powerful. Perhaps all we can say at this stage is that when a conscious experience is taking place, then an event in the brain related in some way to it must have occurred. The brain does not create out of its own physical substance the stuff of consciousness but it may be that it determines in some way we cannot explain what particular conscious state manifests at any particular time.

In the next chapter I want to present some suggestions about other approaches to the relationship between consciousness and the brain.

CHAPTER 7

ALTERNATIVES

'Life like a dome of many coloured glass,

stains the white radiance of eternity'

Shelley Adonais 1821

THE LAND AND THE MAP

Think of an area of land and of the map that covers it. In the land are woods, valleys, roads, towns, a post office, a museum and a youth hostel. These and other features have a parallel on the map of the area: green patches for woods, contours to show altitude, lines continuous or dotted for different types of paths, symbols for the post office and the youth hostel, and so on.

Now consider the relationship between map and land. The land with its features exists before the map is drawn. The map is made in such a way that for each feature on the land that is observed and recorded by the cartographers its counterpart appears on the map.

I have a map of where I live printed over a hundred years ago. It shows a much smaller town, fewer roads, a great expanse of woodland and more farms than are evident on a map of the same area made in the recent past. As the land has changed year by year with more roads, streets, housing estates, factories and so on the cartographers have added more and more detail to each new version of the map. As the features of the land became more complex, so the detail on the maps became more complex.

But always it was the land which changed first and the changes on the map which followed. And always, with every new map, there was the close correspondence, the correlation between the two. The changes on the map came after those on the land. There is nothing new on each revised edition of the map that is not preceded by a changed feature on the land. The map is tied to the land in this regular way. It is not a free floating fiction.

The concept of the land and its map is introduced here to give an illustration of the relationship between the brain and consciousness. As we have seen, there are good grounds for claiming that conscious states are correlated with brain states and that the correlation has a temporal order. The conscious state occurs in response to the brain event. In this simile the land is the state of the brain and the map, closely correlated with the land, represents conscious states.

We understand that a great deal of brain activity, the rapid processing of vast amounts of information, takes place quite unconsciously; in a similar way a great deal of what happens on the land never appears on the map. After all maps, being static objects, do not display, for example, the motion of living beings on the land; furthermore, maps are designed to show only a certain number of all the features on the land. There are particular maps which indicate the relevant features for motorists, walkers, canal users, archaeologists, geologists and so on. So the fact that there is far more going on in the brain than is evident in consciousness tallies well with the map simile.

But like all similes it is not a perfect fit and here is one way in which it gives a misleading impression. In the simile the land takes priority: it exists first and is far more important than the map; indeed the map is merely a means for a better understanding of the land. This is not the relationship between the brain and consciousness. Here consciousness is the primary reality, the seat of all our experiences, feelings, thoughts and ideas. And it may be that the brain serves as the means for the manifestation of consciousness. I will not pursue that claim here since it goes further than we have evidence for at this stage.

THE RADIO

In Chapter 4 I referred to the example of a radio to make a point about causation. I want to develop that idea here. Turn on the radio and hear the music. Turn the dial that controls the volume, first clockwise, next anticlockwise. The music is now loud, louder, now soft, softer. Next move the dial that controls the wavelength. One station after another comes into and out of focus. There is a precise correlation in both cases between the turning of the dial and the volume or the type of sound that is heard. A perfect match.

These dials are part of the radio and the radio is an artifact made of physical components. In complete regularity with how far the dials are turned in one direction or the other, so varies either the loudness or the type of sound that is heard.

Here then we have an excellent example of a very reliable correlation between the radio controls and the sound. But what exactly is the relationship between the two? Is it causal? Well, in one obvious sense it is. What type of sound is heard and its volume are determined by the movement of the dials on the radio. But in another sense the relationship is not causal. The radio does not cause the sound in the sense of creating or making it out of its own substance. An examination of the radio in all its detailed complexity will not bring to light the actual sound. The sound is not in the radio, hidden in some component there. The radio is a receiver and transmitter of sound not a maker of sound. The source of the sound is elsewhere.

I want to suggest here that the radio simile offers another way of understanding the problematic relationship between consciousness and the brain. I hope to have shown earlier two points:

a. that the brain does not manufacture or generate out of itself consciousness
b. that conscious states are regularly correlated with brain states.

What particular conscious state I am in seems to depend on what has happened to my brain. So if I am having an experience of tasting Marmite, there will have been Marmite-information sent from my taste buds to my brain first. If I am having gloomy thoughts about the prospect of going for a walk on a rainy day, I can trace this state of consciousness back to information sent to my brain when I was watching the weather forecast. But neither the taste nor the gloomy thoughts are to be found actually in my brain. There does not seem to be any way whereby the physical stuff of neurons could manufacture the phenomenal feel of sense or emotional experience. Hence the analogy of the radio, a device that picks up what is already present (the radio waves) and emits sound exactly in accordance with its physical state, for example, the precise position of its dials.

The simile of the radio illustrates a model of the relationship between consciousness and the brain. The turning of the dials alters the internal mechanism of the radio. If I turn the volume control clockwise from one position to another, the music becomes louder. These two positions of components of the radio are the occasion for the emission of sound at different volumes. They do not cause the sound itself but the level at which is heard.

It rains a great deal in Snowdonia. The explanation meteorologists give is that clouds moved by the prevailing westerly winds rise over the mountains and precipitate the regular downfalls. The mountains of Snowdonia do not produce out of their rock the water of the raindrops but they are the occasion for the release of those raindrops. The notion of an occasional relationship is distinct from that of a relationship of cause and effect. If I leave a wallet half out of my back pocket, I provide the occasion for a pickpocket to steal it. But it is the pickpocket who causes the theft; my carelessness merely gives him the occasion or opportunity to steal it.

OCCASIONALISM

Occasionalism is not a new model for the relationship between consciousness and the brain. It can be traced back at least to the French philosopher, Nicholas Malebranche, in the generation that came after Descartes. But as a philosophy of mind theory it has now a low reputation. It has often been dismissed as a desperate last ditch attempt to shore up a discredited dualism. Such criticism is unfair and misguided. Occasionalism did not develop as an *ad hoc* lifeboat to rescue drowning Cartesians but was established long before Descartes as a general theory of causation, the problem of the relationship between cause and effect.

One reason why occasionalism has been neglected is that it rests on key assumptions at which many philosophers baulk. For central to traditional occasionalism is the underlying proposition that all causation comes from God, that God is the ultimate cause of everything that happens. It is understandable that, if occasionalism is founded on these grounds, then any enquiry into it needs first to embark on a very circuitous detour into the philosophy of religion before it can grapple with its own particular subject matter of minds and bodies. These two concepts, God's existence and God's total causal power, would need to be demonstrated satisfactorily first, a task that might prove to be a very prolonged and unresolved preoccupation.

For reasons such as these occasionalism has had few supporters and is now presented in philosophical histories as a quaint curiosity of the late seventeenth century like a precisely engineered sextant or an ornate commode, more *Antiques Roadshow* philosophy than cutting-edge analysis.

I hope to make a case for occasionalism as a plausible interpretation of the vexed question of the consciousness-brain relationship without, significantly, any prior assumptions about the existence of God or about the extent of his causal power. But first a digression into the tradition of occasionalism is in order.

OCCASIONALISM: A BRIEF HISTORY

AL-GHAZALI (1058-1111) AND NECESSARY CONNECTION

The notion that the relationship between events in the world around us is occasional is evident in the work of this great Islamic scholar. What is meant by the term 'occasional' is perhaps best illustrated by contrasting it with the notion of necessary connection.

'Necessity' is a key word in philosophy and is drawn from logical links between ideas. If we take one proposition 'George is heavier than Jane', then a second proposition 'Jane is lighter than George' follows necessarily. It has to be that way. Given the first proposition, it is inconceivable that the second is not also the case. Now the idea of necessity is really a feature of the relationship between the two ideas or concepts. We cannot know from these propositions alone whether or not it is actually a fact that George is heavier than Jane. Another way of putting the link is to say that the first proposition (George is heavier than Jane) **entails** the second proposition (Jane is lighter than George).

We can now ask the following question. Are events in the physical world connected with one another in the same way that propositions like the ones above are connected, that is, by necessity? If I put litmus paper in acid, it turns a red colour; if I put a saucepan of water over a gas flame for ten minutes, the water is heated; if I throw a heavy brick hard at a thin window pane, the glass breaks. All very obvious observations. But is the connection between the causes and the effects in these examples a necessary one? Are they connected in the same way that the propositions about the relative weights of George and Jane are connected?

David Hume, the Scottish philosopher (1711-1776), was much exercised by this problem. He argued that there was no empirical evidence of a necessary connection between events and that the idea of such a necessary connection was ultimately a concoction of our imagination. Events to Hume were 'loose and separate'. The idea that events were necessarily connected arose in our imaginations when we saw that one type of event, for example, a billiard ball striking another billiard ball was regularly followed by another type of event, for example, the movement of the second billiard ball.

Many centuries beforehand Al-Ghazali had addressed the same problem. It was essential to Al-Ghazali's idea of God that God could perform a miracle, that God could intervene at any point in time and change the course of events. He took as an example the causal connection between applying a flame to a piece of cotton and the cotton burning. The first event seemed obviously to cause the second event. But was the connection between cause and effect a necessary one in the sense used above? Did the flame coming into contact with the cotton **entail** the burning of the cotton?

At this point Al-Ghazali brings into the discussion God's power to perform miracles. If the flame necessarily causes the cotton to burn, it is inconceivable that burning will not take place when the flame meets the cotton. It just has to be. But if this were true, then God would not be able to intervene by performing a miracle and preventing it taking place. Since God can so intervene, then it follows that the connection between flame and burning cotton cannot be a necessary one. To Al-Ghazali the idea of necessary connection between events would impose a limit on God's power. But God who is omnipotent cannot be so restricted; God can do anything at any time.

Al-Ghazali illustrates his point by an analogy. Suppose a man has been blind from birth because a membrane has veiled his eyes. When the membrane is removed, it is natural to attribute his ability to see to the removal of the membrane. But if we think about the situation more carefully, we understand that the direct cause of his seeing is, according to Al-Ghazali, 'the light of the sun which impressed visible forms on his sight' or, as we might say today, that light reflected from objects around him impinged on his eyes and sent data to his visual cortex (as discussed in Chapter 1). The removal of the membrane (like the scales which St Paul said fell from his eyes) was the occasion for rather than the cause of his seeing.

Al-Ghazali in his analysis of causation was not directly addressing the consciousness-brain relationship. Indeed his work predates by several centuries the mind-body problem as formulated by Descartes and his successors. What is important to point out, however, is that occasionalism as a theory of cause and effect has a long history and should not be rejected as simply a tortuous device to salvage dualism.

NICHOLAS MALEBRANCHE (1638-1715)

George is watching a film of the William Tell story which is just reaching its famous climax. George sees William draw back the string of the crossbow and release the arrow; he sees the apple split by the force of the arrow. George, completely absorbed in the film, identifies with the characters at this dramatic moment. What he thinks he has witnessed, of course, is an instance of cause and effect: the flying arrow causing the apple to split. But if George were to reflect philosophically on his experiences, he might have second thoughts. Cinema is illusion in general but there is a particular type of illusion here that is relevant to occasionalism. When George leaves the cinema, he realises that all the images on the screen throughout the film were caused by light from the projector at the back of the cinema: the projector emitting light that passes through the frames of the film shapes the images of William Tell letting fly the arrow and also shapes the images of the apple being split. It is, strictly speaking, an error to believe that one event on the screen causes another event on the screen.

I hope that Malebranche would have appreciated this discussion of a cinema illusion since it seems to me to capture the essence of some of his teaching. Like Al-Ghazali before him, Malebranche held that there was one source of all causal power, namely God. It may well appear to our senses that one event causes another event (bricks breaking windows and so on) but that appearance is illusory. To Malebranche God is causally responsible both for sending the brick at speed through the air and for shattering the glass. The illusory appearance of cause and effect was a further example to him that the senses are unreliable and do not faithfully represent reality. God is the projector and events are what is shown on the silver screen. We believe that we inhabit a world in which objects move and change one another causally but that view is mistaken. We might think of Malebranche as committed to following through in his occasionalist philosophy the fullest implications of the doctrine of the omnipotence of God, a doctrine which includes the notion that God is the cause of every event that occurs. God is not merely the creator of the laws of nature which can then be left to dictate events in the universe, a view which presents God as a detached, disinterested architect and builder. On the contrary, to Malebranche, God is directly the cause of all events.

But what about conscious events and brain events? According to Malebranche's system God is the power that moves the body (in more modern terms we might say that he was the power that configures the arrangement of neurons in the brain) and God is the power that creates the conscious experience. So when the body is damaged (for example, George stubbing his toe as described in Chapter 1), God both causes the contact between the toe and door and separately causes the pain in the mind of George. The physical event is the occasion but not the cause of the conscious event.

Malebranche also holds that there is an occasional relationship between conscious experiences and brain events in the opposite direction. An intention or choice (the conscious experience) to turn left at the crossroads precedes the movement of the body in a leftward direction (the physical event). To Malebranche there is no direct causal link between the two: both are caused by God and in this case it is the conscious experience which is the occasion for the physical event. Malebranche's occasionalism is two-way.

Occasionalism, then, is a theory of causation which can be regarded as an extension of a particular view of God and the physical universe in which all events are the direct expression of God's will. Despite its emphasis on omnipotence, a key tenet of Christian thinking about God, it has not found favour amongst theologians and philosophers of religion. There may be an interesting reason for this. Advocates of a Christian philosophy are often challenged about the consistency of their view of God and the state of the universe. How can it be, they are asked, that on the one hand God is omnipotent and all-loving and on the other hand many of his creatures experience widespread and intense suffering? Surely, God cannot be both omnipotent and all-loving? For if from his all-loving nature he wishes to eliminate suffering but does not do so, then it follows that he is not omnipotent for a decree of an omnipotent being cannot be resisted. But, conversely, if he is omnipotent and has the power to eliminate suffering but does not do so, then it follows that he is not all-loving for an all-loving God would not allow so many of the beings he has created to suffer so painfully.

A frequent response to this problem is to invoke the idea of free will. According to this idea God has limited his own omnipotence in order to give to his created beings, mankind, the freedom to choose between good and evil. From the free choices of mankind flows the evil (or much of it) that so contaminates the world and causes such suffering. Such a defence of God's all-loving and omnipotent nature is widely held in Christian philosophy.

As you can see, Malebranche's notion of God as the cause of every event that happens is not easy to reconcile with the doctrine of free will which attributes the cause of many events to their source in the free choice of mankind. Understandably, Malebranche's view of causation has not been assimilated into mainstream Christian philosophy.

A NEW OCCASIONALISM

The occasionalism in Al-Ghazali and Malebranche is top-down in this sense: it takes for granted that there exists a God who is omnipotent. Informed by that fundamental intuition, their given, they turned their attention to events in the world and found only the appearance of causation among them. It may well seem that sunlight fades furniture and lawn mowers cut grass but that appearance is illusory. Within this framework the occasionalists identified by reason a sole causal power which is from God.

In the study of the relationship between consciousness and the physical which is the preoccupation of this book no assumptions have been made about God or the causal power of God. The approach has been bottom-up; the analysis has begun with evidence that is immediate and ready to hand and the implications of that evidence have been followed through.

The difference between top-down and bottom-up approaches can be illustrated by reference to the justifications given for religious belief. In the philosophy of religion the truths that are claimed may be reached in two ways: as revelation and by natural religion. Revelation is an instance of top-down knowledge. This view holds that beliefs about God, for example, his powers and the nature of his will, are not known as the consequence of human thought or study like a body of knowledge, the truths of geography or history, for example, but are passed down from God to his chosen representatives to be spread among humanity. The Ten Commandments held to be given directly by God to Moses for the benefit of his own and other people are revelations in this sense. The familiar metaphor of God 'above' suggests the top-down relationship.

Natural religion, by contrast, is bottom-up. It is the attempt by thinkers to use the resources available to them, the power of their reasoning and the evidence of their experience, to construct arguments that purport, for example, to prove the existence of God. There are several instances of such arguments: the design, ontological and cosmological arguments are widely known and studied. And of course the very idea of *constructing* arguments implies a bottom-up approach. Foundations are put down and layers of reasoning built upon them.

The intention here is to present a bottom-up case for occasionalism. I have made no assumptions about God or divine power in this or in preceding chapters. The position reached as regards consciousness may be summarised as follows:

- consciousness is our first certainty and known directly
- the physical is known indirectly
- consciousness is neither identical with the physical nor is it generated by the physical
- conscious states are correlated with brain states
- brain states precede conscious states

If consciousness is not generated by the brain, what then is its source? The raising of this question, it seems to me, marks the limit of the bottom-up approach. The more I pile storey on to storey in the construction, the more the higher levels become rickety and at risk to the strong gusts that blow at this lofty altitude. I am trying to keep within the bounds of reason and not indulge in speculation.

STAINED GLASS WINDOWS

Imagine a church. One of the walls of the long nave has set in it a series of windows. These windows are glazed with stained glass: the colours are red, blue, green and the panes are all manner of shapes: squares, triangles, circles, diamonds. Outside there is bright sunlight. On the stone wall inside the church opposite the windows the sun's rays cast images. Churchgoers see on that wall red squares and triangles, blue diamonds, green circles and many more coloured shapes.

The images on the wall are shaped and coloured by the windows. If you look at the wall, you do not see the light itself but the light transfigured into this patterned mosaic.

We cannot make any sense of the idea of the brain out of itself creating or making consciousness. How could pain and feelings be manufactured from the raw material of neurons? But we observe that consciousness follows the changes in the brain. When a particular brain state is realised, then there is experience of a particular conscious state.

Perhaps consciousness is like the light outside the church. The source of consciousness itself, we do not know directly. But somehow, when the brain is moved into a certain condition, consciousness is expressed in a particular form, a pain, a bolt of fury, a lively idea.

Particular conscious states are like the coloured shapes that appear on the church wall. Just as the colours and patterns on the wall correlate with the windows, so conscious states correlate with brain states.

On this view consciousness exists separately from the brain. It is available to the brain not made by the brain, a potentiality, an undifferentiated state, a capacity in waiting. The brain does not bring it into being but is the occasion for that potentiality to be realised, for that undifferentiated state to manifest in a particular form.

If masons were to renovate the wall to make new windows with different shapes and different colours, then when the sun is bright the churchgoers would see new patterns on the wall.

Maybe, the body is the window that lets in consciousness.

CONCLUSION

In the course of this book I hope to have shown that consciousness is not a temporary anomaly in the all-encompassing physicalist analysis, not the last redoubt holding out against the siege of science. On the contrary, it is the starting-point from which both physicalist analysis and scientific enquiry proceed, not so much the elephant in the room as the room itself. The words of Max Planck are worth repeating: 'Everything that we talk about, everything that we regard as existing, postulates consciousness'.

I am reminded of an old witticism, I forget its source. Coming out of a lecture given by an erudite authority on a subject which might have been anything from physics to theology, a man says, 'Before I heard this lecture I was confused. Now that I have heard it, I am still confused but at least I can say that I am confused at a higher level.'

At the beginning of this book I was puzzled by the nature of consciousness. Now, at the end, after a long study of posited explanations, I remain puzzled. But there is some progress to record: the problem has been clarified, narrowed down to some extent. The argument has been made that consciousness is what we know first and foremost, the immediate certainty, and that particular conscious experiences are in some sort of relationship with matter, more precisely, the neurons in the brain. The nature of this relationship, however, remains a mystery. On the one hand, the neurons in the brain do not manufacture the stuff of consciousness; on the other hand, conscious states, so it seems, manifest only in a correlation with events in the brain. The thesis of one-way occasionalism is to me the most plausible description of the relationship but one that is, to say the least, incomplete.

So many questions remain but a beginning of sorts has been made. There are many areas of enquiry to pursue and no shortage of work that needs to be done.

Printed in Great Britain
by Amazon